D1564623

Domestic Minor Sex Trafficking

Domestic Minor Sex Trafficking

Susan C. Mapp

OXFORD
UNIVERSITY PRESS

OXFORD
UNIVERSITY PRESS

Oxford University Press is a department of the University of Oxford. It furthers the University's objective of excellence in research, scholarship, and education by publishing worldwide. Oxford is a registered trade mark of Oxford University Press in the UK and certain other countries.

Published in the United States of America by Oxford University Press
198 Madison Avenue, New York, NY 10016, United States of America.

Library of Congress Cataloging-in-Publication Data
Names: Mapp, Susan C., author.
Title: Domestic minor sex trafficking / Susan C. Mapp.
Description: New York : Oxford University Press, 2016. | Includes bibliographical references and index.
Identifiers: LCCN 2015049057 | ISBN 9780199300600 (alk. paper)
Subjects: LCSH: Teenage prostitution—United States. | Human trafficking—United States. | Prostitutes—Services for—United States. | Social work with prostitutes—United States.
Classification: LCC HQ144 .M37 2016 | DDC 306.740830973—dc23
LC record available at http://lccn.loc.gov/2015049057

This material is not intended to be, and should not be considered, a substitute for medical or other professional advice. Treatment for the conditions described in this material is highly dependent on the individual circumstances. And, while this material is designed to offer accurate information with respect to the subject matter covered and to be current as of the time it was written, research and knowledge about medical and health issues is constantly evolving and dose schedules for medications are being revised continually, with new side effects recognized and accounted for regularly. Readers must therefore always check the product information and clinical procedures with the most up-to-date published product information and data sheets provided by the manufacturers and the most recent codes of conduct and safety regulation. The publisher and the authors make no representations or warranties to readers, express or implied, as to the accuracy or completeness of this material. Without limiting the foregoing, the publisher and the authors make no representations or warranties as to the accuracy or efficacy of the drug dosages mentioned in the material. The authors and the publisher do not accept, and expressly disclaim, any responsibility for any liability, loss, or risk that may be claimed or incurred as a consequence of the use and/or application of any of the contents of this material.

9 8 7 6 5 4 3 2

Printed by WebCom, Inc., Canada

To my husband Bill Mapp
for all his love and support

Contents

Introduction

Human trafficking is a topic that has grabbed attention in recent years. People are becoming more and more aware that slavery continues around the world. It is currently estimated that there are approximately 21 million people caught in various situations of human trafficking around the world (International Labour Organisation, 2012). Although the majority of media attention is given to sex trafficking, human trafficking includes exploitation for a variety of purposes. Even though the most common purpose is for labor exploitation, primarily agriculture, trafficking for the purposes of sexual exploitation has received the most attention—both in the media and in the judicial system. Although attention was focused initially on those who were trafficked over international borders for sexual exploitation, awareness has slowly increased of the trafficking of US citizens within its own borders, including its children, and legislation has evolved to reflect this. However, due to the still-evolving research on this issue, and the subsequent reliance on mass media, there is a lack of accurate knowledge about this crime that this book seeks to address.

In 2000, the United Nations developed the Protocol to Prevent, Suppress and Punish Trafficking in Persons, especially Women and Children. Also in 2000, the United States passed the first iteration of the Trafficking Victims Protection Act (TVPA; subsequently reauthorized in 2003, 2005, 2008, and 2013). Although trafficking for both labor and sexual exploitation occurs around the world, this book focuses on a subset of those affected: US citizen and legal resident children who are trafficked for sexual exploitation. It was not until 2005 in the third version of TVPA that domestic trafficking was specifically included. As will be discussed in Chapter 1, any person under the age of 18 who performs a sexual act in exchange for anything of value is considered to have been trafficked under the TVPA.

The existence of this crime has shocked and horrified US citizens and galvanized many to want to take action. However, the complexities of this issue and effective ways to fight it have not always been part of the conversation. Many of the people who are doing good work on this issue have been so busy doing this work that they do not have time to write about it. Others have written on these topics, but for a more limited audience. Therefore, the goal of this book is to pull together the knowledge that has been written, in the scholarly literature, popular literature, and mass media, together with knowledge gained from interviews with professionals around the country, in order to distill the best of what we know in order to help guide prevention and intervention services. These interviews have been integrated throughout the text. The list of who participated and their affiliations can be found at the end of the book under the "List of Participants." The knowledge in this field is constantly evolving, and this book aims to summarize what is currently known while recognizing that this knowledge base continues to grow.

To set the stage to accomplish this goal, Chapter 1 introduces the reader to domestic minor sex trafficking—(DMST)-how human trafficking is defined in international and US law and then specifically how domestic minor sexual trafficking fits within this broader category. The chapter discusses what is known about the number of those affected and the limits of those numbers. Macro, mezzo, and micro-level factors that create risk for being trafficked are explored, together with the reasons they create vulnerability.

Chapter 2 goes into more depth about the different forms of domestic minor sex trafficking. Although media depictions focus on pimp-controlled trafficking, there are other forms as well, including gang-controlled, family-controlled, and survival trafficking. The chapter discusses each of these forms—what it is, how it occurs, and the method of selling within it. Chapter 3 then goes on to look at how we can help these survivors exit trafficking. This will vary by type of trafficking, but there are common elements, such as being able to recognize when someone is being trafficked. Different types of professionals, including law enforcement, social service providers, and health care providers, need to be aware how they may encounter trafficking survivors and how best to assist them.

Chapter 4 explores the services that a survivor of trafficking may need in order to recover from the trauma. Providers from around the country were interviewed to learn about what is needed to help these survivors heal. This typically includes case management services such as connecting survivors to medical services, getting them reintegrated into school if needed, vocational opportunities, and many others. Counseling services are also needed, and they must be specifically oriented to the needs of this population. This advanced clinical work must be grounded in a trauma-focused approach and recognize the biological, psychological, and social impacts of trauma.

Chapter 5 looks at what needs to be done in order to stop this crime. There is an increasing focus on the traffickers and the buyers as the perpetrators of crime, as opposed to those who are trafficked. More jurisdictions are using educational programs on the impact of being prostituted to deter buyers. Services to assist those who are trafficked need to be strengthened, and good laws and policies are needed to accomplish these goals. Systems, including criminal justice, child welfare, and social services, need to be coordinated. The last chapter continues this focus by exploring what the everyday citizen can do to fight this crime. There are a multitude of ways in which people can support the good work that is being done.

Readers will note that throughout this book, the word "victim" is never used, but rather "survivor." Tina Frundt, of Courtney's House and herself a survivor of sex trafficking, notes this term is important to indicate the resilience of those who have been trafficked—that they are survivors, rather than victims. Ms. Frundt states that when she is talking with youth, even those who are still in "the life," she tells them, "You survived from yesterday to today. That's something to be proud of!"

This book is written for anyone who wants to know more about this issue and what can be done about it. Although professionals will likely find information that will be useful for them, there is information aimed at the "everyday person" who wants to know more and how to make an impact. There are things that any person can do to help fight this crime and truly make a difference. If you have bought this book, you have already started making a difference, as 10% of all profits from the sale of this book are donated to the antitrafficking organizations My Life My Choice and Courtney's House to help them in their work in fighting human trafficking.

Domestic Minor Sex Trafficking

What Is Domestic Minor Sex Trafficking and Who Is at Higher Risk for It?

The crime of human trafficking was first codified in both US and international law in 2000. The United Nations (UN) developed the Convention Against Transnational Organized Crime in that year in order to have a standard definition so nations could coordinate both their antitrafficking efforts, as well as services to those who had been trafficked (United Nations Office on Drugs and Crime, n.d.). There were three Protocols that supplemented this Convention—the *Protocol to Prevent, Suppress and Punish Trafficking in Persons, especially Women and Children* being the relevant one to human trafficking. It is sometimes referred to as "The Palermo Protocol," although there are actually three Protocols. This Protocol entered into force in 2003 and defines trafficking as follows:

"Trafficking in persons" shall mean the recruitment, transportation, transfer, harbouring or receipt of persons, by means of the threat or use of force or other forms of coercion, of abduction, of fraud, of deception, of the abuse of power or of a position of vulnerability or of the giving or receiving of payments or benefits to achieve the consent of a person having control over another person, for the purpose of exploitation.

Exploitation shall include, at a minimum, the exploitation of the prostitution of others or other forms of sexual exploitation, forced labour or services, slavery or practices similar to slavery, servitude or the removal of organs. (United Nations Office on Drugs and Crime, 2004, p. 42)

In 2000, the United States passed the Trafficking Victims Protection Act (TVPA) for the first time. The definition in the TVPA is quite similar to the UN definition and includes trafficking both for sexual exploitation and labor exploitation, though not organ trafficking. A commercial sex act is defined as any sex act when anything of value is given or received (US Department of Health and Human Services, 2012, para. 3).

Sex trafficking*: the recruitment, harboring, transportation, provision, or obtaining of a person for the purpose of a commercial sex act, in which the commercial sex act is induced by force, fraud, or coercion, or in which the person induced to perform such act has not attained 18 years of age; and*
Labor trafficking*: the recruitment, harboring, transportation, provision, or obtaining of a person for labor or services, through the use of force, fraud, or coercion for the purpose of subjection to involuntary servitude, peonage, debt bondage, or slavery. (US Department of Health and Human Services, 2012, para. 3)*

When defining human trafficking, there are three essential elements: act, means, and purpose. *Act* is what is done (i.e., recruitment, harboring, transportation, provision, or obtaining), while *means* is how it is done (i.e., force, fraud, or coercion). *Purpose* is why it was done (i.e., for sexual or labor exploitation). It is essential to note that according to the TVPA, force, fraud, or coercion is not required to establish trafficking if the person is under 18 years of age.

Perhaps due to the term "trafficking," there is continued confusion about whether movement is required for trafficking to exist. However, movement is not required as noted by the word "or" in describing the Act. People can be, and are, trafficked where they live. There is also often a focus on trafficking across international borders, perhaps due to the fact that the UN Convention includes the word "Transnational." However, according to the International Labour Organisation (2012), the majority of those who are trafficked do not move at all and only 30% are transported across an international border.

Understanding has evolved over the years regarding where trafficking exists and who is affected. Originally, trafficking was seen as something that happens in less developed nations to their citizens. Then, it was seen as something that did occur in the United States, but mainly to citizens of other nations. Only recently was it realized that it occurs with citizens of this country. As stated by Melissa Snow, child trafficking specialist for the National Center for Missing and Exploited Children, "We have plenty of vulnerable women and children within our communities unfortunately; this is who traffickers are targeting. Why would they focus overseas when they can spend a lot less money, time, and effort reaching into our own communities?"

Reflecting this evolution of understanding, it was not until the 2005 reauthorization of the TVPA that the trafficking of US citizens and legal residents was specifically included in the law. This 2005 reauthorization noted that runaway and homeless youth are at particularly high risk, and it established funding for domestic survivors, including a pilot program for residential facilities for juveniles (Annitto, 2011). However, it was the report by Shared Hope International in 2009 that first coined the term "domestic minor sex trafficking" to signify the specific population that is the focus of this book: children who are US citizens or legal residents who are trafficked within the country for the purpose of sexual exploitation. There has been exponential growth in awareness of the existence of this crime since that time; however, there continues to be considerable confusion about what exactly it includes and who is affected by it. Media portrayals have resulted in a stereotype of a White suburban girl who has been kidnapped and held captive by a pimp. This stereotype is damaging because its narrow focus does not include the vast majority of trafficked youth and thus they are not identified and assisted.

This stereotype also often results in youth being seen as passive actors in this crime, as reflected in the names of governmental programs to assist them such as "Rescue and Restore" and "Innocence Lost." By failing to see that youth often regard themselves as active agents in the decisions that led to the trafficking situation (as discussed in later chapters), assistance may not be offered to youth who are not seen as amenable, or assistance may be rejected by youth who do not see themselves as needing rescue or able to be rescued. The term "rescued" has in fact fallen out of favor and the Federal Bureau of Investigation (FBI) will typically say "recovered" currently (e.g., FBI, 2014).

Domestic Minor Sex Trafficking

As noted in the TVPA, anyone under the age of 18 years engaging in sexually related activities in exchange for something of value—such as money, drugs, food, or shelter—has been trafficked, regardless of whether force, fraud, or coercion exists. This includes all forms of sexual activity— prostitution, stripping, and pornography—as well as what has been termed "survival sex," in which a person trades their body in order to obtain basic needs, such as food or shelter. This definition of trafficking as any child involved in the commercial transaction of their body renders terms such as "juvenile prostitution" outdated, as there is no longer such a thing as children under 18 years consenting to sell themselves. However, as will be discussed, this unfortunately conflicts with state and local laws still on the books, as well as public perception, and these children often do find themselves treated as criminals.

There are four basic types of domestic minor sex trafficking in the United States: pimp control, gang control, familial, and survival (these will be explained in detail in the next chapter). However, this does not mean that permutations do not exist or that youth cannot move between these types. There are no reliable statistics regarding the number of children who are sexually exploited in the United States due both to the hidden nature of the crime as well as arrest of the children themselves for not only prostitution but also for other crimes such as assault, drug charges, or running away. As discussed by Salisbury and Dabney (2011), estimates of this crime are vulnerable to what is termed the "Woozle effect," in which one researcher states an estimate, but notes the limitations of how that figure was derived, but subsequent citations remove the qualification and the estimate evolves to be considered fact.

The two most cited statistics of the scope of domestic minor sex trafficking are that each year, an estimated 300,000 children are at risk of being trafficked and 100,000 are in situations of trafficking. The 2001 report by Estes and Weiner is the source of the 300,000 statistic, and it is based on data gathered from published research, service data from national agencies serving homeless youth, other previous research on "sex for money" and their own field research on "sex for money." It is important to emphasize that this statistic is an estimate of those at risk for 17 different categories of commercial sexual exploitation of children, and it is not an estimate of those experiencing it, which the authors state would be a different type of study (Estes & Weiner, 2001). Additionally, this study was released in 2001 before widespread use of the Internet by children, and selling of sex online, and thus that element was not included at its full potential current impact.

The 100,000 figure comes from testimony to Congress by Ernie Allen, then CEO of the National Center for Missing and Exploited Children. He derived this figure based on the Estes and Weiner study as well as other studies available at that time (Allen, 2010). However, the methodology for the development of this figure is unknown, and thus it should be regarded with caution. Despite the almost complete uncertainty about the validity of these figures, they are widely used, typically with their cautionary methodical notes removed—what is known as the Woozle effect.

The 2009 Shared Hope International report also attempted to gain a sense of the scope of the issue utilizing rapid assessment methodology. However, due to its reliance on data from interviews with professionals and arrest records, it is believed to seriously underestimate the scope of the problem (Dank, 2011). Despite these limitations, this report helped bring to light many of the barriers to addressing domestic minor sex trafficking, including identifying its survivors as criminals, a lack of appropriate services, and lack of attention to addressing demand (Shared Hope International, 2009).

Despite the uncertainty of the number of children who are trafficked, a task force convened by the Institute of Medicine (2013) stated that it was not a good use of resources to determine an exact number, that this effort would be better put toward actually solving the problem rather than determining exactly how many people are affected by it. To try to solve it, we need to understand why it occurs and what risk factors increase its likelihood—societal, familial, and individual.

Societal Factors

There are a number of factors in US society that help to create an environment in which children are sold for sex. Several of the interviewed

providers discussed issues of racism, sexism, and classism as contribu-
tors to trafficking. We live in a society in which many people struggle to
meet their basic needs, where there are more barriers to success for
those who are non-White, and where traditional gender roles still
proliferate. To draw out one example, a great deal of research has
examined the sexualization of females in media and its impact. The
American Psychological Association Task Force on the Sexualization of
Girls (2007) found vast evidence of the sexualization of both women
and girls in all forms of media. In advertising, there has been a dis-
turbing trend in which ads use sexualized images of young children or
emulate child pornography in their ads (Smith, Herman-Giddens, &
Everette, 2005).

Children have a high exposure to media. Those between 8 and
18 years of age spend an average of 7 ½ hours each day consuming media
content—TV, Internet, video games, cell phones, and such; this does
not include texting, which is an additional 1 ½ hours every day. Those
with the highest use are young teens (11–14 years of age) and African
American and Hispanic youth (Kaiser Family Foundation, 2010). These
are also the groups at the highest risk for trafficking. As this study was released in 2010, this exposure may be even higher today. One 2015 study
by Common Sense media found an average of 9 hours of media use each
day by teenagers (Tsukayama, 2015).

Exposure to sexual content in media has been found to increase teen
sexual activity and raise the risk of coercive sexual victimization (Ybarra,
Strasburger, & Mitchell, 2014). This study excluded the sexual content
that is easily accessible on the Internet, including through cell phone use.
Children learn very early from these media messages that one can get
attention through appearing sexy. They also learn that there is a particular type of female body type that will gain them this attention. This
has a broad variety of impacts on girls, including social and emotional
consequences such as increased shame, anxiety, and even self-disgust,
as well as reduced ability to focus and concentrate. Mental and physical
consequences can include eating disorders, low self-esteem, and depression; these media images can also hinder the ability to develop a healthy
sexuality as an adult (American Psychological Association Task Force on
the Sexualization of Girls, 2007). Heteronormativity in media could also

increase feelings of stigmatization in lesbian/gay/bisexual/transsexual/ queer (LGBTQ) youth.

Technology appears to have played a role in the increasing sexualization and availability of sexual images. Pornography is readily available on the Internet, and "sexting" is now a common term. There has also been an acceptance of "pimp" and "ho" language within society, beginning with MTV's show "Pimp My Ride," which began the use of *pimp* as a verb and then expanding to airlines, websites, and other reality shows (Coy, Wakeling, & Garner, 2011). Popular music also includes these ideas, such as the song "It's Hard Out Here for a Pimp," which won an Academy Award. One law enforcement officer noted:

It's glorified now to be a pimp, you look at the TV shows, "Pimp my Ride." Pimp this, pimp, it's in songs, everything is pimp, pimp, pimp, and so when these guys do that, you've got these . . . girls who don't know any better and they'll think it's cool and they'll hang out with them, and they'll start smoking with them and after that they'll say, "Oh you want to try it?" "Yeah, I'll try it." (Dank et al., 2014, p. 69)

In some cases, this normalization has caused girls to regard involvement in the commercial sex industry as an easy way to make money and to seek out men to serve as pimps for them. If the youth live in neighborhoods with others who are selling sex, they notice that these sex workers also seem to have money and take cabs everywhere (Kennedy, Klein, Bristowe, Cooper, & Yuille, 2007). A quarter of the pimps interviewed by Dank et al. stated that they had started in the business due to recruitment by women. However, even if workers initiate the relationship, they still do not receive much of the money they earn (Dank et al., 2014).

In addition, it has been argued that the presence of the adult sex industry, legal or otherwise, perpetuates the idea that it is permissible to purchase people to meet one's sexual desires. The infantilization of adult women in this industry then feeds the desire for those who are actually children. When Amnesty International stated that they were exploring a policy statement calling for the full decriminalization of sex work (subsequently adopted), Sex Trafficking Survivors United (2014), an international coalition of survivors and survivor-led organizations, issued a statement vehemently against this idea. They stated:

It was shocking for us to see Amnesty's suggestion that it is a "human right" for well off, powerful (mostly white) men to purchase the bodies of the younger, poorer and more vulnerable. We found it especially cruel that Amnesty says prostitution is a choice. (para. 3)

Thus, a society in which there are pervasive images of females portrayed as sexual objects leads to the internalization that this is an acceptable role. Including children in this sexualization increases the acceptance of children as sexual objects as well. All of this contributes to a society in which the selling of children for sexual pleasure is accepted.

Familial and Individual Risk Factors

While almost all US youth have been exposed to these societal factors, there are familial and individual factors that can increase the risk. Specific experiences appear to place children at higher risk of being trafficked than others, including previous abuse, family dysfunction, and poverty. Although these factors will be discussed separately, it is important to note that they often overlap and affect each other.

However, it is essential to emphasize that being trafficked for sexual exploitation is something that can, and has, happened to all types of people. All the professionals interviewed for this book emphasized this point. Bonnie Martin, a therapist in Alexandria, Virginia, who works with survivors of trafficking, stated:

I've worked with exploited kids from home-schooling Christian conservative families, and I have worked with trafficking survivors who have endured terrible poverty and live in housing projects. I have had middle-class clients. I have had clients who graduated from college and clients in master's degree programs. Sex trafficking can happen to anyone, anywhere. It knows no bounds.

Race, sex, and gender

Children of all races are recruited. Some pimps believe that White girls can make more money, while other believe that non-White girls are more appealing due to a desire for the "exotic." Some pimps believe that White and Asian girls are better able to blend into their target markets, while some Black pimps believe that it raises red flags to law enforcement if they are with anything other than Black girls (Dank et al., 2014). In short, children of all races are targeted, albeit for different reasons. While media images tend to portray only White girls, in actuality African American youth appear to be at the highest risk, especially African American boys (Reid & Piquero, 2014).

While much research and media attention is focused on girls as those who are affected by sex trafficking, and many providers serve only girls, boys are survivors of this crime as well. There are a number of reasons why there is not as much attention or awareness given to boys who are experiencing this crime. One is that we are not looking for it. As noted by Holger-Ambrose, Langmade, Edinburgh, and Saewyc (2013), since services tend to be oriented toward girls and research studies tend to draw from those accessing those services, girls will be more likely to be included in these studies and thus counted. In addition, even when studies acknowledge that males are trafficked, they still are very likely to focus only on girls (Dennis, 2008).

Boys are often excluded from consideration and, as a result, from services. Melissa Snow of the National Center for Missing and Exploited Children (NCMEC) states that a large percentage of the sex-trafficked children they see have been girls, but "This does not accurately reflect the actual picture of who is being victimized. Instead, it reflects who media attention and some antitrafficking groups have focused on in raising awareness, including trainings and informational materials. And that directly impacts who professionals, such as law enforcement, are viewing as victims of sex trafficking and how they're applying that." Supporting her view, a number of studies have found relatively high numbers of boys who have been commercially exploited for sex. Dennis (2008) reviewed 166 articles relating to those working in the sex trade and found that the vast majority of them excluded any mention of males. Those that did include them ascribed them more power over their situation than females and made the assumption that the main threat to their well-being was HIV, rather than violence. Additionally, their sexual orientation was often questioned, while this was not true for females.

In contrast, when studies are population based and not focused on sexual exploitation, boys tend to be equally represented with girls as survivors of trafficking. For example, in a study focused on the prevalence of exchanging sex for drugs or money, as opposed to prostitution or trafficking, the researchers found that two thirds of those who had done so were boys (Edwards, Iritani, & Hallfors, 2006). Community-based studies of trafficking led by Dank have found that approximately half of their participants were young men: 54% and 47% (Dank, 2011; Dank et al., 2015). The 2015 sample was only about one-third female (36%) due to the sizable transgendered sample (as discussed later in this chapter, members of the LGBTQ community are at higher risk for being trafficked than their peers). One community study in Norway found that boys were three times more likely to have had sex for money than girls (Pedersen & Hegna, 2003). Reid and Piquero (2014) found that of all children, African American boys were at the highest risk for experiencing commercial sexual exploitation. Thus, there are a substantial number of trafficked boys who are typically overlooked or ignored.

Part of this exclusion may be a result of our gender norms around boys and girls. Girls are to be the recipients of sex, while boys are the initiators. Girls are cast as needing protection, while boys are supposed to be the protectors. If boys are the protectors, they cannot be victims. This was seen in sexual assault laws that for years defined sexual assault as only occurring to females. Dennis (2008) purposely reflected these norms in the article titled "Women are victims, men make choices"—subtitled "The invisibility of men and boys in the global sex trade." Showing the impact of these norms, police are more likely to arrest boys involved in selling sex than girls (Moxley-Goldsmith, 2005).

These gender expectations not only prevent policymakers, service providers, and law enforcement from seeing boys as exploited, but they also prevent the boys from seeing themselves that way. Boys may choose to view themselves as entrepreneurs who are "hustling," in order to feel they have power in the situation (Estes & Weiner, 2001). Similar to girls, boys often become engaged in commercial sex in order to meet their basic needs. Like females, they typically have high rates of previous sexual and physical abuse and lack family support (ECPAT USA, 2013).

The stigma surrounding homosexuality in the United States can also contribute to a lack of identification of exploited boys. Many boys do not want to admit that they have been engaging in these activities, especially if they themselves do not identify as gay (sometimes known as "gay for pay"). Whether or not they themselves are gay, if they have been having sex with men, they may fear being labeled or stigmatized by staff. Among those boys who have been identified as sexually exploited, there is an overrepresentation of gay or transgendered boys, and they frequently note that they were thrown out of their house for their identity (discussed later in this chapter).

Age of Entry

Various research studies have found varying ages of entry, most of them in early adolescence; for example, 12 (Ashley, 2008); "by 13" (Holger-Ambrose et al., 2013); 16 (Raphael, Reichery, & Powers, 2010). As will be discussed in Chapter 2, those who are trafficked by family members are typically trafficked at younger ages. Adolescents, due to their developmental stage, are at higher risk of trafficking. Adolescence has long been known to be a time of thrill-seeking, a lack of thought regarding consequences, impulsive behavior, and a desire to expand boundaries regarding independence and freedom. Developments in neuroscience and understanding of brain development have begun to help us learn about the biological base for this.

Historically, it had been believed that brain development was limited to prenatal and early childhood stages of development. However, recent research has found that the brain continues to evolve until early adulthood and undergoes a significant reorganization during adolescence (Konrad, Firk, & Uhlhaas, 2013). As a result, the ability to make well-thought-out decisions is still developing in adolescence. The prefrontal cortex, which controls areas such as control of behavior, planning, and risk assessment, matures later than the areas governing other tasks (Konrad et al., 2013). The frontal lobe does not fully develop until the twenties, thus inhibiting the capacity to make logical, rational choices. Teens tend to have more difficulty anticipating negative consequences than adults or seeing more than one option in a situation, and they tend to attach higher value to the potential rewards of risky behavior, particularly under times of stress (Beyer, 2011). Adolescent brains also react differently to the anticipation of a reward than the brains of either adults or of children; they have a greater activity in the nucleus accumbens than the other age groups, and this activity is correlated with risk-taking behavior (Blakemore & Robbins, 2012; Konrad et al., 2013). Sensation seeking rises during this period of development (Romer, 2010) and adolescents tend to have a preference for actions that produce an immediate reward (Blakemore & Robbins, 2012). While adolescents are cognitively able to rationally assess a situation, the more developed limbic and reward systems will prevail over the relatively immature prefrontal cortex in emotionally laden situations.

These "emotional situations" tend to be ones in which there is the anticipation of a reward or those that occur in front of their peers (Blakemore & Robbins, 2012; Konrad et al., 2013). The social context has a powerful effect on adolescent behavior. Whereas the prefrontal cortex is most underdeveloped in early adolescence, the more dangerous behaviors occur for most teens as they age into their early twenties, emphasizing it is not the brain development alone that creates the risk, but this in combination with what is going on in their environment and what their peers are doing (Willoughby, Good, Adachi, Hamza, & Tavernier, 2013). This can help explain why knowledge is insufficient to dissuade teens from risky actions (Arden & Linford, 2009). The knowledge of these influences is evident in driving laws that limit the number of peers that a teenage driver can have in the car.

Optimal brain development is impeded by exposure to trauma, maltreatment, and severe stress during childhood. The National Scientific Council on the Developing Child (2012) notes that an infant's brain develops based on a "serve and return" model. An infant reaches out to a caregiver through babbling, gestures, and facial expressions, and most caregivers respond in kind. However, neglected infants do not receive the expected response—it may be "unreliable, inappropriate or absent" (p. 1). The Council states that this not only inhibits the ability of the brain to learn how to form connections with others but also causes a stress response. The chronic washing of the brain in stress hormones affects the brain architecture and results in long-term difficulties in such areas as academics, social functioning, and mental and physical health. Chronic neglect inhibits the long-term ability to deal with adversity and is associated with poor impulse control, lower self-confidence and self-esteem, and social skill deficits, all of which increase the risk of trafficking.

Other forms of maltreatment also cause detrimental changes in the brain architecture. The trauma of child abuse can cause physical changes in the brain that impede emotional and behavioral functioning. Survivors of child sexual abuse have been found to have changes in such brain regions as the cerebrum, the corpus callosum, the amygdale, and connections with the limbic system, causing difficulties in understanding and regulating emotion, underdeveloped empathetic abilities, increased aggression, and increased impulsivity (Reid & Jones, 2011). Experiencing any type of abuse, though not neglect, is also associated with increased scores on an assessment of novelty seeking (de Carvalho et al., 2015).

The spindle cells in the brain that help us process information quickly and assist in self-control and the ability to sustain attention are not likely to have received the needed stimulation and thus may be underdeveloped in cases of early maltreatment (Arden & Linford, 2009). Spindle cells likely also help with a person's ability in relating to others and processing emotions (Arden & Linford, 2009). As children who have been maltreated have more difficulty processing emotions, especially positive and neutral emotions (Young & Widom, 2014), they will have more difficulty assessing and detecting risk in a person who may be attempting to traffic them.

Poverty

As mentioned in the discussion of societal factors, living in poverty in the United States increases an individual's risk of being trafficked, though it certainly affects those from all socioeconomic classes. Growing up in an impoverished family is a risk factor for a variety of reasons, including biological, psychological, and sociological factors. Similar to the impact of trauma on the brain, growing up in poverty has been found to negatively impact the developing brain, particularly in regions that affect academic success and decision making (Noble et al., 2015). This direct impact is also mediated by exposure to stressful life events (Luby et al., 2013).

The developing brain can also be impacted by environmental factors. For instance, those living in poverty, especially in urban environments, are more likely to be exposed to lead (Hawthorne, 2015). Magnetic resonance images (MRIs) have found that lead exposure as a young child causes physical changes to the brain. These changes have numerous detrimental cognitive and behavioral effects on the developing child that could increase the risk to later trafficking, including lower intelligence quotient (IQ), higher impulsivity, academic difficulties, and more attention difficulties (Hawthorne, 2015; Wright et al., 2008).

Those who are living in poverty are more likely to be raised in an area where they know people who are involved in selling sex, either themselves or facilitating the selling of another. A major factor in being recruited into the sex trade is knowing someone who is involved, be that a family member, someone from the neighborhood, or from school (Dank et al., 2014). Lack of economic opportunity can be a push factor into sexual exploitation. The youth may feel they need to make money somehow in order to help support their family. They may also feel pressured by our consumer society that they need certain material items. Due to their physical location and their circumstances, they likely lack other ways to make money, or if they do manage to make money, it is not a substantial amount.

In other cases, rather than simply their own survival, it might be the survival of the family for which the youth is earning money. Youth living in poverty might find commercial sex to be the easiest way in which to earn money to help their family pay the bills (Dank, 2011). Youth growing up in distressed areas do not have a lot of options to earn decent money. Sex work may be the only option to earn needed funds. One study found that youth stated that they remained involved with sex work due to the high amounts of money they were able to make and were proud of their abilities to earn these amounts. However, despite this described income, all but one participant in this study described themselves as homeless. The researchers noted in their discussion that it appeared to them that the participants used the "illusion" that they were earning this money to mask the "painful truth that they were being exploited" (Holger-Ambrose at al., 2013, p. 335).

Poverty disproportionately impacts those who are not White. This intersection can further increase the risk of trafficking. Racial minorities are disproportionately more likely to live in poverty and attend substandard schools. The institutional racism within the criminal justice system also makes minority youth more likely to have a criminal record, impeding their access to the job market. Amelia Rubenstein of TurnAround in Baltimore notes the impact of the intersection of race and class issues on risk factors for trafficking on her clients.

I had a kid who I talked to who was making hundreds of dollars every time she stripped and she's 13 years old. Now, there's a lot of stuff going on in her family. However, she also comes from one of the poorest neighborhoods in Baltimore, which is one of the poorest areas on the East Coast. She doesn't have a pimp. That kind of money is

so much higher above anything else she would be able to make, and
she comes from a community where young women primarily do not
have economic opportunities, so that type of money speaks worlds. . . .
I think it's really easy to ignore the economic components of this and
not talk about it as a poverty, class, and race issue, and it absolutely is.

Family Dysfunction

Family dysfunction has been found to be common among those who are trafficked—though this should not be assumed to be a universal experience; children from what are seen as "good" families are also trafficked. If children's families does not meet their needs, this can place children at higher risk for being trafficked (Macias-Konstantopoulos, Munroe, Purcell, Tester, & Burke, 2015). Experiences of abuse and neglect, parental substance abuse, and parental mental health issues have been found to have been experienced by many of those who have survived trafficking (National Scientific Council on the Developing Child, 2012; Nixon, Tutty, Downe, Gorkoff, & Ursel, 2002; Williamson & Prior, 2009). These issues and others can lead to lack of needed parental supervision. Parents working long hours to earn money for the family may not be able to be there to supervise their children. Parents may also be caught up in their own issues or activities, including substance use.

Children who have a family member with a substance use problem are at higher risk for being trafficked (Clarke, Clarke, Roe-Sepowitz, & Fey, 2012; Reid & Piquero, 2014). Among juveniles arrested for prostitution, those who themselves use drugs report lower levels of parental control and supervision than their non-drug-abusing peers (Brawn & Roe-Sepowitz, 2008). This family dysfunction and experience of abuse can lead to a child being placed into foster care, another known risk factor.

Having experienced maltreatment as a child appears to greatly increase the risk of being trafficked. Although not every maltreated child will be trafficked, professionals interviewed noted that the vast majority of their clients had been abused as children: emotionally, physically, and/or sexually. Their experience is supported by extensive research. Widom and Kuhns (1996) found in a prospective cohort study that girls who had been maltreated, especially if they had been sexually abused or neglected, were significantly more likely to be selling sex as an adult compared to their non-abused peers. The same was not true for boys in this initial study. However, a later analysis of this data set found that all types of maltreatment increased the risk of prostitution of an adult. This appeared to be due primarily to the fact that maltreatment tended to lead to earlier sexual initiation, but it also increased the likelihood of other risk factors, including running away, committing a crime, and having problems at school (Wilson & Widom, 2010). A review of the literature by Lalor and McElvaney (2010) in noting this linkage between childhood sexual abuse, especially penetrative sexual abuse, that has been found in a number of studies states that there may also be mediating factors such as family dysfunction that increase the likelihood of both sexual abuse and later sexual exploitation.

This linkage may be due to lessons that maltreated children learn. Children who have been abused have learned that people who love you mistreat you. Emotional abuse teaches children that they are of low worth and that those who say they love them and are supposed to care for them will demean and disrespect them. Those who have been emotionally abused have been found to be significantly more likely to experience sexual exploitation as children and to experience it at a younger age than other children (Roe-Sepowitz, 2012).

Children who are physically abused have learned that physical violence is an expected part of a loving relationship. Furthermore, if they have been sexually abused, they learn that their body does not belong to them, that it exists for someone else's pleasure. These children also learn to keep secrets and hide information from authorities (Lankenau, Clatts, Welle, Goldsamt, & Gwadz, 2004), a required skill while trafficked. Beth Bouchard, of the Support to End Exploitation Now coalition in Boston, notes, "I think when someone's been sexually abused previously, it teaches them that their body doesn't have worth, or that their worth is through sex, that they don't have control over their body, that it's not theirs." Abuse teaches children that they do not have the right to say no (Howard, as cited in Smith, H. A., 2014) and that they cannot control what happens to their bodies. One survivor stated that she initially believed that prostitution was a way to regain the control that had been taken from her by the experience of childhood sexual abuse (Nixon et al., 2002):

When you're sexually abused, I always thought I had control over the men. I never thought about it as they're using me. I always thought

*I had the power. The more money I made, the more wanted and loved
I felt because I always associated love with sex. (p. 1024)*

———————

Attempts to get away from the maltreatment can then create additional risk factors, including being placed in foster care, running away, or
joining a gang. Maltreatment has been found to increase the risk of joining a gang, especially for girls, possibly in search of the loving family not
found at home. Exposure to violence, both at home and in the community, can also increase this risk because youth may seek safety and protection from the gang (Kerig, Wainryb, Twali, & Chaplo, 2013). As noted in
Chapter 2, gang-involved trafficking is on the rise.

Experiencing abuse can increase the likelihood that children will run
away. In their study of youth on the street (half boys, half girls), Gwadz
et al. (2009) found extensive experiences of maltreatment; over three
quarters had been emotionally abused, while two thirds each had experienced physical abuse, emotional neglect, and physical neglect. About 40%
had experienced sexual abuse, but this rose to two thirds among the girls.
Another study found that among girls who were homeless or had run
away, experiencing sexual abuse when they were young increased their
likelihood of later sexual victimization in several ways. It affected it directly, as well as increasing other risk factors that then, in turn, increased
the likelihood of later victimization. These other factors include having
friends who sell sex, trading sex for survival needs such as food or shelter
(survival sex), and being on one's own at an earlier age than girls who had
not been victimized in this way (Tyler, Hoyt, & Whitbeck, 2000).

To protect maltreated children, some may be removed from their
family and placed in foster care. However, this can create another set of
risk factors.

Foster Care

Children in the foster care system are extraordinarily vulnerable to being
trafficked. Numerous studies have found high rates of having been involved with the child protection system among youth who have been
sexually exploited (e.g., Macias-Konstantopoulos et al., 2015; Nixon
et al., 2002; Williamson & Prior, 2009). According to Melissa Snow of
The National Center for Missing and Exploited Children (NCMEC), in
2014, 68% of the endangered runaways who were reported to NCMEC

and found to be exploited through sex trafficking had been in the care of foster care or social services when they went missing. In a nationwide raid conducted in 2013 by the FBI, 60% of the youth recovered from trafficking had been involved with the foster care system (NPR, 2013). As Withelma "T" Ortiz Walker Pettigrew (2013), sex trafficking survivor and alumna of the foster care system, stated in her testimony to Congress:

Youth within the system are more vulnerable to becoming sexually exploited because youth accept and normalize the experience of being used as an object of financial gain by people who are supposed to care for us, we experience various people who control our lives, and we lack the opportunity to gain meaningful relationships and attachments. (p. 6)

Children come into the foster care system when they have been confirmed as being maltreated by their caregiver and are no longer safe at home. This might be due to physical abuse, emotional abuse, sexual abuse, or neglect. The most common reason children are identified as maltreated is neglect—their basic needs, such as shelter, food, and clothing, are not being met (Children's Bureau, 2014). Poverty is a clear correlate of neglect. As discussed, these all raise the risk for being trafficked. Additionally, when traffickers work to recruit these children through gifts and small luxuries, they are at a heightened vulnerability to be swayed by these tokens.

Once in the foster care system, too many youth are in foster homes with caretakers who do not truly care about them. Ms. Pettigrew stated that caregivers often use the support money from the state to purchase luxuries for themselves, and the youth are told they are simply the means to a paycheck. Thus, even before they are trafficked, these children are being taught that their purpose is to bring money into a household (Pettigrew, 2013). Additionally, children may be abused while in foster care (Lankenau et al., 2004; Pettigrew, 2013), reinforcing the message that their bodies belong to someone else. An advocate reported that a survivor stated that for her:

Foster care was the training ground to being trafficked. She understood that she was attached to a check. And what she points out

is that at least the pimp told her that he loved her, and she never heard
that in any of her foster care placements. (NPR, 2013, para. 11)

Due to these experiences, many youth in the child welfare system will run away from their placement. There are certain characteristics that make a child in foster care more likely to run (see Box 1.1). The draw of biological family and connections with those who care appears to be a factor in the risk of running. Courtney et al. (2005a) described this as "their hope to connect with others whom they believed cared about them and understood them" (p. 5). This may explain why children who were removed at an earlier age are less likely to run, as are those who are placed with family. Courtney et al. (2005b) stated, "Many youth reported feeling as though they had been on their own since they entered the system. They saw their running as a quest for what they believed was missing in their lives" (p. 50).

Though youth may recognize that their families are not ideal, they regard being in a birth family as "normal," and like most teenagers, crave normalcy (Courtney et al., 2005a). Human development is primed for children to be raised in a family. For those who are unable to be raised by their biological family and/or are not getting the nurturing they need from that family, they will often seek out a replacement. Courtney et al. (2005b) note that:

In the absence of a connection to a biological family, many youth
attempted to "create" family in various ways in order to access the

---

BOX 1.1 Risk Factors for Running Away From Foster Care

- Girl
- Non-White
- Older (14 years and older)
- Removed from birthfamily at older age
- Not placed with family (together with sibling or in kinship care)
- In residential care
- Higher number of placements

Sources: Courtney et al., 2005a, 2005b; Coy, 2009; Lin, 2012.

sense of connectedness, support, and guidance they thought they
needed . . . these young people deeply and openly long for a family
structure, particularly parental figures. (p. 54)

In relation to trafficking, if children believe that the traffickers care about them, and they do not believe that anyone else does, they will run away in order to maintain that relationship. Indicative of this desire for connections, youth were far more likely to run from residential care, as compared to either a foster home or a kinship placement (Courtney et al., 2005b), though this may also be due to the level of care the child is perceived to need.

As they age, children experience the natural adolescent yearning for control over one's life and this chafes against these strictures, which can result in the youth running from placement. The typical adolescent desires for freedom, autonomy, and adulthood are also present in these youth, but their atypical experiences can exacerbate these drives. They typically live in an environment that limits their ability to make decisions for themselves and practice autonomy; the child welfare system is not designed for individual decision making (Courtney et al., 2005a). Children in the foster care system have even less say over what happens in their lives than their same-age peers. Their lives are dictated by their caseworkers and foster parents. Especially if they are in a residential center, the type of placement from which youth are most likely to run, they do not have the same freedom of movement as their peers.

While these youth have less decision-making ability than their peers, at the same time, they frequently feel more able than other teens to make these decisions since they have frequently had to grow up faster than average due to their maltreatment (Courtney et al., 2005a). Courtney et al. (2005b) note running satisfies "the desire to have a sense of autonomy and independence that they remembered having while living in their families and communities of origin" (p. 65). The adolescent drive for independence may be driven by the evolutionary need to break away from the family of origin in order to find an acceptable mate (Konrad et al., 2013).

In addition to these common factors and issues related to their developmental stage, Courtney et al.'s study (2005b) found a group of youth, especially girls, who would run at random, for no apparent reason. This group tended to have experienced traumatic events both in their families of origin as well as in placement and to have longed for a life free of worry and stress. They felt un-cared-for and unattached and would leave without warning. They may have been invited to go away by a stranger or friend, and they tend to be gone for extended periods of time and stay with strangers, especially adult men. This group is clearly at high risk for being trafficked.

When children in foster care go missing, there often is not a major effort to find them, unlike a biological child. Melissa Snow of NCMEC has had child welfare workers tell her that they attempt to report a missing foster child to local police, only to be told to wait a certain period of time (e.g., 24 hours) before officially reporting it, despite the fact this is against federal law. According to federal law, law enforcement agencies may not require a waiting period of any kind, and a missing child must be entered into the National Crime Information Center (NCIC) within 2 hours of receiving the report. NCMEC has the ability to work across jurisdictions and has a 97% recovery rate. NCMEC has a specialized team focused on child sex trafficking with full-time analysts who work around the clock to locate these children. They have access to a large number of resources and specialty skills that law enforcement can call in and request assistance.

Runaway and Homeless Youth

Although children who have been maltreated are at high risk for running away, any youth who has run away and/or is homeless is considered to be at very high risk for being trafficked (Macias-Konstantopoulos et al., 2015). NCMEC believes that one out of eight endangered runaways reported to it in 2012 experienced sex trafficking. Of these children, two thirds were in the foster care system when they went missing. They are overwhelmingly female, but that is likely more to do with who is being reported than who is actually in the population. Traffickers know that those who are homeless are vulnerable, and they know where the homeless shelters for youth are located. The shelters can hold only a certain number before they are full; subsequent seekers of shelter must be turned away. One service provider noted that traffickers will wait outside the shelter, stating it becomes like a "shark tank." They wait for the youth to be turned away and then approach them as a friend and offer to help with offers of food or shelter.

Although estimates vary greatly, there are believed to be between 1 and 3 million youth on the street (Colby, 2011), who are there for a variety of reasons. In addition to fleeing abuse or the child welfare system, they may be escaping bullying at school or other factors that made life at home unbearable to them. Others have been "pushed out" by their families (sometimes termed "throwaway" children). This may be due to lack of acceptance by their families (as described later for sexual minority youth), high levels of family conflict/dysfunction, or other reasons. Federal statistics state that up to 75% of cases of youth who have left home are not reported by their families due to anger at the child or relief that the "problem child" is gone (Urbina, 2009). An FBI operation in 2014 that recovered almost 170 children from sexual exploitation found that many of them had never been reported as missing (Tucker, 2014).

Once on the street, youth are at high risk for a variety of negative consequences, including mental health difficulties, not attending school, and high-risk behaviors such as substance use and sex with multiple partners and/or unprotected sex (Colby, 2011). They may also experience violence while on the street. All of these factors make them extremely vulnerable to being trafficked as they are seeking to reduce these risks. Although this is true for all youth, sexual minority youth can be at even higher risk of being trafficked due to a variety of factors.

Sexual Minority Youth

Approximately 40% of homeless youth are reported to be a member of the LGBTQ community (Durso & Gates, 2012). Gwadz et al.'s (2009) sample of homeless youth found that about half identified as other than heterosexual, including 22% of those born biologically male who identified as trans*. These rates, much higher than those found in the general population, make it clear that these youth are at much higher risk to be on the streets. This is often due to stigmatization and rejection—at school, at home, within the child welfare system, and other places.

There is a high level of harassment of LGBTQ youth in school, which can cause them to run away or be vulnerable to recruitment. The 2011 School Climate Survey by the Gay, Lesbian & Straight Education Network found that 85% of those surveyed had heard biased remarks at school, including 57% who heard them from teachers or other staff members. Eighty-two percent were verbally harassed, and 38% were physically harassed. Almost one third of the sample had skipped a day of school in the preceding month because they felt unsafe or uncomfortable at school. This harassment impacted students' grade point averages (GPAs), post-graduation plans, and levels of depression and self-esteem.

In addition to harassment at school, these youth are at higher risk of being pushed out of their homes due to lack of acceptance by their families. Durso and Gates (2012) found that more than two thirds of service providers for homeless youth stated that family rejection was a major factor in the homelessness of the LGBTQ youth that they served, the most common factor cited. The National Center for Transgender Equality (2011) also found family rejection to increase risk for involvement in sex work; 19% of those who reported that they lacked familial acceptance had performed "sex work or other underground work for income," as compared to 11% with familial support.

Sexual minority youth are significantly more likely to have been involved with the child welfare system than sexual majority youth (Irvine, 2010; Wilson & Kastanis, 2015). Once in the system, they continue to face difficulties due to discrimination, including rejection by foster parents, verbal and physical harassment, and hostility (Clements & Rosenwald, 2007; Urban Justice Center, 2001, as cited in Yarbrough, 2012). They report poorer treatment by the child welfare system, a higher number of foster care placements, are more likely to be placed in a group home, and are more likely to be homeless (Wilson & Kastanis, 2015).

Clements and Rosenwald (2007) found that all but one of the foster parents in their study who had knowingly had a gay youth placed with them had asked to have that youth removed because of this factor. This was due to misconceptions such as that the youth was likely to molest their own child or feeling it violated their religious beliefs and thus would damage their reputation. Gay boys were regarded with more fear than bisexual or lesbian youth. Rejection by foster families then leads to multiple placements and ending up on the street due to being pushed out or running away, often due to the youth's safety concerns (Urban Justice Center, 2001, as cited in Yarbrough, 2012).

Once on the street, LGBTQ youth can face even higher barriers to survival than other homeless youth. They may be turned away from shelters or harassed within them due to their sexual or gender identity (Dank et al., 2015). In one study of transgender adults, it was reported that 29% had been turned away from shelters due to their identity, 55% were harassed by shelter staff on this basis, while 22% were sexually assaulted by shelter staff or residents (National Center for Transgender Equality, 2011). Shelton (2015), in interviewing transgendered homeless youth, found that they reported a number of systematic barriers in shelters, including a lack of affirming programs, staff members who lacked knowledge regarding their particular needs, and a lack of privacy. This made them feel unwelcome and thus unsafe.

Children With Disabilities

Children with disabilities can be at higher risk for trafficking due to the difficulties associated with their diagnosis—whether a cognitive disability or learning disability. Children with learning disabilities are at higher risk for involvement in the criminal justice system (Beyer, 2011), and the risk factors can translate to risk of being trafficked as well. Some of these diagnoses inhibit the youth's ability to process information or to strategize, making them more vulnerable. Youth with attention-deficit/hyperactivity disorder (ADHD) or attention-deficit disorder (ADD) are characterized by their impulsivity and distractibility, as well as difficulty with social skills, which can place them at risk (Beyer, 2011).

An area that has not been explored much is how those with a developmental disability may be at risk for being trafficked. They may create an ideal candidate for the trafficker as they may be biologically mature, and in some cases over 18 (thus the penalties of trafficking a child are not applicable), but mentally they are much younger and thus more easily deceived. It can also be more difficult for the police to interview these youth and get information from them for prosecution. Twill, Green, and Traylor (2010) published a description of girls at a residential center for those who had been trafficked and found that 60% had been assessed as having mild to moderate mental retardation. The authors noted the limitations of this finding—a small sample, the weaknesses of intelligence assessment, and the possibility of selection bias—but it should open the door to further exploration of this issue.

Tina Frundt, founder and executive director of Courtney's House in Washington, DC, states that her agency has worked with several girls who had autism. The trafficking recruitment can happen in a variety of ways, including online or at school. As children with autism have a very concrete concept of the idea of a "friend," if they believe someone is their friend, they trust that person and may introduce them to others with autism. They also have a very concrete idea of what a trafficker is—they are mean people, and if someone is nice, then that person cannot be a trafficker. A case review of 70 trafficked girls by Reid (2014 found that 14 of them (20%) had intellectual disabilities. They tended to be targeted by traffickers at the school bus stop or when leaving their house. Similar to what was noted by Ms. Frundt, they are likely unable to understand the difference between a boyfriend and a pimp.

These children may also be trafficked by someone at school. This can be an adult, such as a teacher or staff person, or it may be another student. For example, in some school districts, children with autism are placed in a school for special education that shares a building with an alternative school, including students who were placed there for emotional and behavioral concerns, including those who are gang affiliated. They are then recruited and trafficked by their classmates.

Conclusion

This chapter has provided a broad discussion of how domestic minor sex trafficking is legally defined and who is affected by it. It also outlined experiences and influences that can make youth be at a higher risk for being trafficked, though as noted, trafficking can happen to anyone, regardless of upbringing, socioeconomic status, sex, gender, sexual orientation, or any other demographic category. The next chapter will outline the main categories of methods of trafficking, including how children are recruited and exploited.

2

Methods of Domestic Minor Sex Trafficking

Although the popular press has primarily focused on trafficking by a pimp, there appear to be four main methods of domestic minor sex trafficking: pimp controlled, gang controlled, familial trafficking, and survival trafficking. These methods can be fluid; survival sex can turn into trafficking by an exploiter and vice versa (Covenant House, 2013; Dank et al., 2015). When adult women were asked who recruited them to begin selling sex, the rates were approximately equal for the types of people identified: pimp, family member, friend, and self (Kennedy, Klein, Bristowe, Cooper, & Yuille, 2007). Thus, although pimp-controlled trafficking receives the most media attention, it is by no means the only type. In fact, one study found it to be in the minority of types of trafficking; in their sample, regardless of whether the person entered the commercial sex trade as a youth or as an adult, it was far more likely for them to have been brought in by a peer or a customer. This was especially true for transgendered youth (Marcus, Horning, Curtis, Sanson, & Thompson, 2014). Regardless of the type of trafficking, the buyers are almost all the same: adult men.

Pimp-Controlled Trafficking

Pimp control is the type about which the most is known, and it primarily affects girls. In the majority of these cases, a girl is sold by an individual man, though female traffickers are by no means unknown. This man may have other girls working for him, one of whom he may have promoted to assist him, often known as a "bottom girl." Although in some cases these girls may have been kidnapped and forced to work for him, in the vast majority of cases, they are lured in, either by him acting as a friend or a boyfriend or by one of the girls working for him. The trafficker is typically an adult, but again not always; children have been found to be trafficked by same-age peers as well (Reid, 2014).

Research has found that the majority of those at the "high end of the market," that is. $60 to $120 an hour, are being trafficked. As law enforcement notes, even those who say they are on their own ("renegade") are, in fact, not. They are told to say that no one is controlling them, but this is often not the truth. Minors cannot get credit cards to place online ads, nor can they book a hotel room. Therefore, an adult must be doing those things (Dank et al., 2014).

Although trafficking by a pimp primarily affects girls, service providers noted that it also affects boys, especially gay boys. They can be contacted on the Internet, such as in chat rooms or on Facebook, by someone they believe to be a potential boyfriend. This person then lures them in the same way as will be described for girls. Thus, while the pronoun "she" will be used in the following section to reflect the majority of cases, this should not be taken to suggest that this form of trafficking does not occur with boys as well.

Recruitment

Traffickers work to locate youth who seem vulnerable for some reason— abused, bullied, low self-esteem, on the streets—a variety of the issues discussed in Chapter 1. They will then groom the youth for a period of time before turning them out. Grooming is the process through which the pimp gains the trust of the youth and builds a bond with them so that later when they seek to turn them out into selling sex, it will not be so difficult. It also reduces the likelihood of the child being willing to testify against the trafficker due to the bond that is created (Reid, 2014). Grooming involves psychological manipulation. The groomer may use flattery, gifts, money, or sexualized behavior to draw the youth in. Child sexual abusers groom children in a similar process. In that literature, a definition of grooming has been developed that fits grooming for trafficking as well:

_____

A process by which a person prepares a child, significant adults and the environment for the abuse of this child. Specific goals include gaining access to the child, gaining the child's compliance and maintaining the child's secrecy to avoid disclosure. This process serves to strengthen the offender's abusive pattern, as it may be used as a means of justifying or denying their actions. (Craven, Brown, & Gilcrest, 2006, p. 297)

_____

Use of the Internet can make the recruitment and grooming process easier for pimps. Facebook has been a common means for pimps to locate and lure girls. They are able to reach out to many more vulnerable youth, and if their profile is not set to "private," the youth's vulnerabilities are there for the world to see: a fight with their parents, feeling unaccepted at schools, low self-esteem, and many others. The pimps can look through their pictures and discover what they like to do in order to start a conversation. The recruiters can send mass messages and see who responds. They then carry on conversations with whoever does respond. To build a perceived connection between them and the youth, they will match the youth in how they communicate and what they are interested in, for example, beliefs, interests, experiences (Whittle, Hamilton-Giachritsis, Beech, & Collings, 2013). Several law enforcement agents noted the use of the Internet as a recruitment tool. Donna Gavin, lieutenant in the Boston Police Department and the commander of the Human Trafficking Unit, states one of the major methods of recruitment is:

_____

Kids getting on Facebook, just meeting up with strangers. It's sad to say, but I was talking to kids the other day, the bottom line is, if it sounds too good to be true, it is. If you're walking down the street and somebody says to you, you're so beautiful, do you want to be in a movie, do you want to make a video ... this really happens and these kids fall for it. So I think anyone is at risk, but I think it's kids that these guys know to prey upon. I think it's really kids with lower self-esteem, maybe having no support, no family, looking for love kind of

thing. Most of these things start out as a boyfriend. These guys are very
clever and they know the things that the girls are lacking or looking for.

It is not just that the person with whom they are chatting is unknown that increases risk, but children's behavior is different in a virtual environment. They often feel safer online, both physically and psychologically, and this can serve as a disinhibiting factor. They can be more likely to talk with a stranger, which they have been trained not to do in person. Whittle et al. (2013) discuss this, reviewing the literature supporting this finding, noting that physical invisibility and asynchronous conversation seem to reduce inhibitions. Additionally, many youth have no supervision of their online activities. These factors combine to make youth more likely to take risks with online behavior that they would not take in real life (Whittle et al., 2013).

Special Agent Louis Morlier of the Department of Homeland Security notes that it is not just chatting on Facebook that creates risk but also chat rooms through providers such as Yahoo and Moco Space, which allows chatting on cell phones. He notes that parents are becoming increasingly aware of the need to monitor their children's computer activity, but they are not necessarily aware of the chatting ability on cell phones. He believes this increased ability raises the risk of trafficking.

The need to go out and find a runaway out of place, who looks
vulnerable, is less necessary now because of chat rooms and social
media. The would-be trafficker can now find those who are vulnerable
simply by what they are saying in the chat room and seduce them
entirely through communications on the Internet and talking them into
meeting somewhere. Then the child disappears.

This method of recruitment is seen in the following case study discussed by Fink and Segall (2013):

Nina was a middle-class high school senior who was preparing to
head to college when her mother was arrested and sent to prison for
two years. Her plans derailed, Nina felt out of balance and uncertain.
She started received Facebook messages from a man and began a

friendship. He told her he was falling for her and they made plans for their future including marriage and children. In September, when her friends went to college, Nina went to Seattle to meet him. Almost immediately, he dropped her on the street and told her it was time to make money. She felt she had no one at home to turn to and thought he loved her, so she stayed. He used physical violence to maintain compliance, but her shame aided in that; she couldn't imagine returning home to tell her family what had occurred. Eventually, she was recovered through a raid and is now receiving assistance to heal the trauma she has experienced and go to college.

———————

Recruitment occurs in other ways as well. In some cases, pimps place job ads on the Internet, stating they are hiring for models. They may even have an office space with a secretary to conduct interviews (Dank et al., 2014). Others recruit in person, such as at the mall, the beach, or other places youth hang out. They may walk past a group of girls and say, "Hey beautiful!" and see who turns around. If a girl turns around, to him that signals that she is seeking that external validation of her worth and may be vulnerable to his recruitment. One pimp stated that he looked for a group of three girls and would target the second most attractive, as he believed the most attractive was immune to the attention and the least attractive would be suspicious of it. However, the middle girl, used to being in the shadow of her more attractive friend, would be susceptible (Kennedy et al., 2007). A common phrase for girls heard from multiple sources is, "You're really pretty. You could make some money."

Once the initial connection is made, he will then groom her. He may act as her boyfriend, buying her nice things, spending money on her, and taking her places. He may also act as if he were able to fulfill her youthful dreams such as being a singer or model (Williamson & Prior, 2009). One law enforcement official explains it in the following manner:

———————

When they start recruiting, especially with young girls, pretty much what they do is go and give the girls an ear ... and the girls end up telling them, "I am having this problem at home, my mama is doing this, and my dad is not doing that." And they will just figure out what is going on with this girl and they will fill that void. At first they might not even approach her with the prostitution or anything like that. They just want to take her and shower her with what she is missing: gifts, attention or whatever. Once he gets her away from her family and it has been some time, he will eventually approach her and be like, "Take care of my man for me." And he might ease her into it or he will tell her, "Baby, we cannot live here for free. There are bills that need to get paid and everything, you need to start contributing." Well, of course she does not know how to contribute so he tells her she can do it for a short period of time, we can get this money and then we can go get this big house or whatever and they will go for it. (Dank et al., 2014, p. 79)

However, pimps report that the most common way that they recruit is through their own social networks and in their neighborhoods. The youth may be approached by someone they know, a friend of a friend or someone from their neighborhood. By utilizing this connection, it can overcome the initial caution about an unknown person. By recruiting in impoverished neighborhoods, it increases the likelihood that the person needs money, as discussed in Chapter 1. This alternative person may also be in charge of the grooming process (Williamson & Prior, 2009). See Table 2.1 for "persuasion tactics" used by pimps.

However, it should be noted that in some cases, the pimp does not recruit directly. He may have one of his "girls" do it for him in order to overcome that initial fear that a girl may have about a strange man. The girl may be offered an incentive for every new recruit she gathers (Dank, 2011). One study of women controlled by pimps found that while 25% stated they had been recruited by a woman, only 6% had a female pimp at the time of the study (Raphael, Reichert, & Powers, 2010).

As noted in the first chapter, those who have been abused are at particularly high risk for being recruited. Lisa Goldblatt Grace, cofounder and director of My Life My Choice in Boston, notes that girls in a group home, juvenile justice facility, or group shelter may bring a more naïve, younger, sometimes cognitively limited girl with them when they run away, and thus bring that girl into the life. The pimps prey on the need for love and affection and pretend to meet it. They will pretend to be a friend or a boyfriend to these girls and buy them nice things and fulfill material desires that they have (Hom & Woods, 2013; Reid, 2014). This builds her

Table 2.1 Persuasion Tactics

Tactic	Features
Romantic or sexual relationships	Often used to recruit individuals not previously engaged in sex work; appeals to individuals' emotional needs
Mutual dependency	Emphasizes the benefits of a pimp–sex worker relationship; encourages concept of shared, day-to-day subsistence
Monetizing sex	Encourages women to get paid for activities they were already engaged in; often used to exploit women in economically vulnerable situations
Associated lifestyle	Verbal promises of material comforts; outward display of wealth and business profits
Reputation	Pimps build reputations around how they treat and take care of employees; generally helps attract individuals interested in or already engaged in sex work

Source: Dank et al. (2014, p. 167).

trust in the pimp and creates an affection bond. Later, if the pimp uses violence to break her down, it is not unknown to her because this is what she experienced growing up and will not flee from it.

Smith (2014), a survivor of domestic minor sex trafficking who has published a book about her experiences, notes that in her case, the "breaking down" process began long before she met her trafficker. She had already been accustomed to the concept of trading sex for needs, that her body was an object. She states that this occurs not only through personal experiences such as abuse and assault, but through popular media images promoted in songs, movies, advertisements, and so on, reflecting the influence of these media images discussed in Chapter 1.

Children who have run away or been pushed out of their homes are at very high risk of recruitment, as discussed in Chapter 1. They will often flee to the city, but then not know where to go or how to survive. Pimps or a bottom girl will wait around a bus station looking for those children who get off the bus, but then appear lost. They will befriend them and offer assistance—a place to sleep, food to eat. In some cases, they may wait around shelters and other organizations serving homeless youth in order to recruit them. Shelters can only hold a set number of people, and once they are full, youth will be turned back on the street and be vulnerable to recruitment. This extended recruitment process, with its psychological manipulation, is often referred to as "finesse pimping" (Dank et al., 2014).

Turning Out

With finesse pimping, after the initial period of grooming, which varies greatly in length of time, the trafficker will tell the youth that it is time to "give back" and coerce them into selling sex, known as "turning out." For those who recruit in the role of a boyfriend, they may state that the youth needs to pay them back for the gifts they were given, or the trafficker may pretend that they themselves owe a debt to someone and they need the youth's help to earn the money to pay it off. They may also pretend that this debt is due to the gifts they have been giving the youth. Another tactic seen is a weekend trip to another city without the knowledge of the youth's parents. The pimp will pretend to have a financial emergency; he will state that he needs money immediately and then talk the youth into selling sex to earn the "needed" cash (Kennedy et al., 2007). This can also happen with those who recruit through another type of relationship to the youth, such as caregiver or friend, as discussed in the following two examples from the work of My Life My Choice.

Jessica had a bad home life. Her mother and father were using drugs, her father was abusing her mother, and they both were abusing her. Her friend, a seventh-grade boy, said she could live with him and his mom. His mom said, "Yeah, come on over, you can stay with us." So Jessica lived with them for a period of time and someone took care of her and nurtured her and cared for her. She was then driven to a hotel and told it was now time to pay them back.

Amanda was bullied throughout middle school. When she got to high school, an upperclassman said, "I'll protect you, I'll take care of you, you don't need to have this happen." He developed a trusting relationship with her and protected her from the bullying, and then he started selling her to his friends after school.

The trafficker will work to weave a web of psychological and physical coercion in order to maintain control over her. For the men who recruit as a boyfriend, they often encourage the idea that she is part of a new family by having the girls to refer to him as "Daddy" and the other girls as a "wife-in-law." Especially for girls who were raised in a dysfunctional family or who experienced abuse, this replicates what they have come to expect from a family. One of the girls may be raised up to be the "bottom" girl and given authority over the other girls. She is not equal to the pimp, but is above the others and may be in charge of recruitment and grooming. Bottom girls are often seen as more culpable by law enforcement, but they themselves have been psychologically manipulated. This complicity also may be the only way for them to avoid exploitation and abuse themselves.

These dynamics help keep a girl from simply walking out. She feels dependent on the pimp. She has come to view him as the source who can meet her needs. He provides food, shelter, and clothing, as well as occasional gifts and treats, such as a manicure. The trafficker may then state she owes him money for this and coerce her into "working off the debt" (Reid, 2014). This can occur through telling the girl that she needs to earn money to repay the initial things she was given, including clothes, food, or shelter, making this an obligation she must fulfill (Williamson & Prior, 2009). He provides love and attention, though because that typically wanes after he turns her out, it then puts the girl in the position of feeling she must work to please him in order to regain that. One study found that pimps explicitly stated that they use "manipulation, emotional abuse, exploitation of vulnerabilities and encouragement of dependencies" in order to build and maintain control over the girls (Dank et al., 2014, p.171). They use a variety of methods of psychological coercion, including that he is still a boyfriend and/or that she is doing this to earn money for "them," for their life together.

The pimp also typically reinforces the idea that she is a criminal, that she is choosing to sell herself. Once she is turned out, the pimp tells her that no one will accept her anymore, that she is a "whore" and selling her body is all she is good for. Thus, the girls do not see themselves as crime victims, but as crime perpetrators, and thus unaccepted by society and those who care about them.

Girls will often be constantly monitored, especially at the beginning. They are often isolated, by movement to another city, or by having their own phone taken and replaced by a phone monitored by the pimp (Reid, 2014). The pimp may also threaten their family (Hom & Woods, 2013). Some pimps will use violence and threats of violence right from the start and are known as "gorilla" pimps (sometimes spelled "guerrilla"). These threats of violence may be aimed at the youth, their friends, or their families (Kennedy et al., 2007).

Regardless of the initial type of trafficker, all may use violence or the threat of violence if she attempts to rebel. A girl might hear stories from the other girls of what happened to a girl who would not comply, tried to keep some money for herself, or who did not meet her quota for the night. This can include beatings, rape, and starvation (Hom & Woods, 2013). Some girls state that they remain affiliated with their pimp because he helps protect them from the violence they risk by being on the street, even while noting they experience violence at his hands (Holger-Ambrose et al., 2013). Pimps may feel that the girls are a reflection on him, and thus he may use violence to keep them under control (Dank et al., 2014). Some will beat those under their control for no reason, but simply to remind them of who is in charge and to keep them too scared to leave, including the use of a "pimp stick," an unbent and doubled-over coat hanger (Kennedy et al., 2007).

Raphael et al. (2010) found that in their study of pimp-controlled women, a quarter stated they were subjected to violence at the time of recruitment, but this rose to 75% when asked about the experience of violence by the pimp at the time of the interview. Similarly, half reported experiencing coercion at the time of recruitment, but 60% at the time of the interview. There was a correlation between levels of violence and coercion, and those who were younger were more likely to experience higher levels of coercion.

The pimp may also get them addicted to drugs in order to create another bond (Hom & Woods, 2013). Drugs can also be used as a way to make the act of prostitution easier or the girl more willing (Holger-Ambrose et al., 2013). This, however, varies from pimp to pimp as some pimps prohibit drugs. They want the girls clean as they believe that those who are addicted to drugs are more difficult to control (Dank et al., 2014).

There may be rules that the girls must follow. Rules often include that if they are walking the track (selling themselves on the street), they can never look another pimp in the eye. This can be construed as "choosing up," signaling that she wants this other person to be her pimp. This rule may be extended to the idea that she cannot look any African American male in the eye, based on the stereotype that they are all pimps (Dank et al., 2014; Williamson & Cluse-Tolar, 2002). Girls cannot walk on the sidewalk if a pimp is walking by them; they must step off, sometimes referred to as "Pimps up, ho's down" (Smith, 2014). They also often have a nightly quota that they must meet; the youth is not finished for the night until he or she has earned the amount specified by the pimp, regardless of how long it takes (Williamson & Cluse-Tolar, 2002).

Means of Selling

Girls are sold through different means, the most common of which are by the Internet, word of mouth, or on the street. Other electronic means of selling include chat rooms and phone. More "old-fashioned" methods might include newspaper advertisements or the Yellow Pages, placed under the Massage Services section (Dank et al., 2014). Craigslist shut down its adult services section in 2010 due to pressure; however, other sites such as Backpage still allow these ads. While Craigslist will remove the ads when they are discovered, the pimps just keep posting them in order to reach the buyers (Dank et al., 2014). While typically Craigslist takes them down almost immediately, one ad in a study was left for 27 minutes, during which time the researchers received 14 contacts from buyers (Roe-Sepowitz, Hickle, Gallagher, Smith, & Hedberg, 2013). Agent Morlier notes:

Although Craigslist is officially against trafficking, with tools like RSS feeds, a trafficker only has to put the ad on for a few seconds to get the word out. So even if Craigslist takes it off, the message went out. And those who are willing to pay for it [sexual services] still get the email with the number.

Selling on the Internet has shifted much of the earlier street-based activity indoors (Dank et al., 2014). While officially the ads are only allowed for adults (those over 18) to advertise, in reality there is no method to check this. Law enforcement and advocates peruse these ads looking for clues that the person is underage. Some of these clues include that the photo was taken in a hotel room, that the girl is making the "duck face" (a face that younger girls believe is sexy), or simply that she looks young.

A 2012 study by Dr. Roe-Sepowitz, a professor of social work at Arizona State University, and Lieutenant Gallagher of the Phoenix Police Department found that 80% of the ads on Backpage in their study were for adult services Department (Roe-Sepowitz & Gallagher, n.d.). As Backpage charges a higher amount for these ads, this is clearly a huge moneymaker for them (Summers, 2013). While Backpage has rules and teams that screen ads, they appear ineffective. Roe-Sepowitz and Gallagher identified 88 potential minors in their study that they referred to the Vice Squad, none of whom had been identified by Backpage. The identifiers they used were as follows:

(1) Subjects in the photos had physical indicators of youth to include, but not limited to, child-like fat on cheeks, little to no curve at the waist, feet/legs outturned when standing, gangly arms and legs.

(2) The environment where the photo was taken had features indicative of common juvenile behavior to include, but limited to, writing on the mirror, stuffed animals, posters on the wall, and animals in the photo.

(3) The photos were staged as if the subject of the photo was intentionally trying to look young or was made to look young through the appearance of pigtails, stuffed animal being held, wearing knee high socks and holding school books.

(4) The ad indicated the subject of the photo was potentially a juvenile through the use of verbiage to include, but not limited to, "barely legal," "just turned 18," "first time." (para. 11–14)

In some cases, these youth will be sold in one city, while in other cases, they will be transported from city to city. The pimp will advertise them ahead of time and set up "dates" in that city prior to their arrival. For example, the I-95 corridor on the East Coast includes a number of major cities in which pimps can sell. Miami is on a circuit with other major cities, including Atlanta, Dallas, and Houston (Dank et al., 2014). Moving around has a number of advantages for the pimp. It allows their "product" to be rotated so there is something new to offer the buyer; it keeps the girls from becoming comfortable; and it and allows them to reduce their chance of detection by law enforcement, particularly the likelihood of minors being spotted by law enforcement. They will network with other pimps who know that city to learn how to avoid law enforcement (Dank et al., 2014). Pimps may also trade girls among themselves. If a girl is causing problems, they may trade her. If she is from the area, and they want to remove her from her supports, they may trade her (Dank et al., 2014). Special Agent Morlier notes:

They use the Internet and personal electronic devices to market the trafficking victims with much greater ease and to a much broader area than what was available in the past. Their mobility has increased because they can market to such a large area and that makes it difficult between jurisdictions. Coordination of any sort of a response in a timely manner remains a challenge. They're willing to go anywhere that there is a transient male population willing to pay for the service. They tend to market to truck stops with truckers and military bases with military members. But there's also a component that provides sexual services anywhere someone can access the Internet and has a desire. Anyone who has some sort of sexual deviance that they don't feel comfortable bringing to a normal partner and is willing to pay someone to access a person, they [the traffickers] are going to provide that service.

I think the traffickers are, based upon what I've seen, as mobile as they need to be. If they find an area where there's little effort at enforcement, they will tend to stay there because they can build up a customer base. If they perceive a lot of enforcement, they may rotate to other counties and even other states and work a circle with a long enough period of time between contacts, so they might just stay under the radar of local law enforcement's attention. So they can adapt to the amount of scrutiny that law enforcement is committing to the problem.

Truckers are considered a prime market for the selling of sexual services because they are typically male and often drive long distances and are thus away from home. Although they do encounter adults who are not under the control of another person, they are also likely to be solicited by youth who are. The child will go to a truck stop and go from truck to truck, knocking on the doors, looking for a person interested in purchasing them. The youth are also taught how to use the CB radio to solicit customers (Williamson & Prior, 2009).

These children are also sold on the street. They may walk a "track" or "stroll," an area where they offer themselves to those driving by. Although this presents a security risk for the pimps because they cannot control the environment and the girls may be at a higher risk of experiencing violence or encountering law enforcement, there is a constant demand from buyers because they know where to go. As one pimp noted, rather than waiting for a call to come in, they are out actively engaging with buyers (Dank et al., 2014). Another pimp felt that the increased danger on the street increased the girls' dependency on him.

Gang-Controlled Trafficking

The awareness and occurrence of gang-controlled trafficking have been growing. Gangs—local, national, and international—have become aware of the enormous amount of money that they can make through the selling of sex. After all, a drug can only be sold once, but a person can be sold hundreds of time. If a person is found with drugs, this clearly signals a crime to law enforcement, but if he is found with a girl, there is no such indicator. Additionally, drug trafficking requires start-up funds to purchase a quantity of drugs large enough to sell, whereas no such investment stream is needed for sex trafficking. Girls are not a finite resource, and there are no issues with Border Control. Thus, it is seen as "high yield and low risk," according to Detective Bill Woolf of the Fairfax Police department and head of the Northern Virginia's antitrafficking task force (2013). Quite often, the families of these girls do not know they are being trafficked. In some cases, they go to school long enough for attendance to be taken and then leave. In other cases, they will be at school the whole day, be sold after school, and be home by seven, or they will sneak out after bedtime.

While gangs are traditionally associated with urban areas, they have been spreading to suburban and rural areas as well (Cole & Sprang, 2015; Lederer, 2011). Transnational gangs, such as MS13, national gangs (e.g., Crips), and local gangs (also known as crews) have all been known to engage in sex trafficking. For the transnational and national gangs it can be primarily to make money, while for the local crews it is also a means to establish their identity and reputation (Woolf, 2013). The extent to which gangs participate in human trafficking varies from area to area. For example, in San Diego, it is rare for Latino gangs to engage in sex trafficking because they state it is contrary to their values to make money off their women (Dank et al., 2014). However, in the Washington, DC, area, transnational Latino gangs are known for their participation in this crime (Woolf, 2013). Rival gangs have even been found to cooperate with each other in order to facilitate sex trafficking (Dank et al., 2014).

Gangs are both similar and different from pimps in their methods of recruitment and control. Both are primarily focused on girls because it is primarily men who are the buyers, and there is a large stigma associated with homosexuality in gangs. In some cases, recruitment methods will mirror that used by pimps with grooming methods or befriending runaways. For example, Lisa Goldblatt Grace notes that at her agency, the recruitment methods of befriending and grooming have remained the same, but that the proportion of the exploiters who are gang members has been growing. In other cases, such as when recruiting within their own territory, they will "snatch and grab"—kidnap girls off the street who are already in the life (FBI, 2012).

Social media is a primary method of recruitment by gangs as well as pimps; it is more time effective; they can send messages to 40 girls rather than talking with just one or two face to face. It also creates deniability; members will claim, "It wasn't me," when asked about messages sent from their account. False accounts can also be set up (Woolf, 2013). Because the gang members are often young, they will also use their personal networks to recruit from local schools and neighborhoods, as well as local malls, beaches, or anywhere that young people hang out (Dank et al., 2014). Gangs may hold "skip parties" in which they throw parties during school hours. The youth attend school until attendance is taken for the day and then leave (Frundt as cited in Smith, 2014; Patel, 2013).

Deepa Patel, of the Multicultural Counseling Center in Fairfax, Virginia, and clinical consultant on gangs and trafficking, states that gangs will often use girls to recruit other girls. Similar to bottom girls, this girl will work to befriend a lot of other girls, typically seeking out those they feel are vulnerable, such as knowing they have been sexually abused or lack supervision. Ms. Patel's coworker, Tesy Molina, notes that girls are often attracted to gang membership for the same reasons as boys: "They want the sense of identity, the sense of belonging. They want to feel loved. They want to feel like they're a part of something." Ms. Patel notes the kids are drawn to gangs because of the relationship that is offered. It meets their needs that may be developmental, such as fun and excitement, needs that could be for survival, such as food and shelter, or psychological needs, including a feeling of belonging, identity, and/or prestige. As noted in Chapter 1, girls may also join gangs as way of seeking safety from maltreatment at home or in the community.

"Recruiters" will then take the girl through a grooming process, inviting her to come and hang out with them and their friends. It will then progress to inviting her to have some drinks with them and then to having sex with one person, and then another. The recruits will then be told, "Hey, you could make money doing this," to put that idea in her head. Gangs may also use the equivalent of a gorilla pimp, in which he will offer shelter to a runaway only to have her raped repeatedly once in his home.

Gangs are also similar to pimps in that they seek to re-create the dynamic of a family, which many of their members lack. However, it is more complex with gangs due to the number of members. Rather than one man who is "Daddy," they are seeking to replace the whole family (Woolf, 2013). They recruit girls, who then think they are part of the gang. However, some gangs, often the international gangs, do not truly accept girls as members, viewing them as weaker and "snitches." For gangs that do accept girls, they can be "jumped in" (beaten) or complete a mission, same as the boys, and then have the same status as a boy. However, girls may also be "sexed in," that is, sleep with a gang member. This gives her membership, but at a lower level, and she is never viewed as a full-fledged member (Kerig et al., 2013).

Gang loyalty is developed with the mentality of "gang over all." These girls, and other members, are indoctrinated to believe that the most important thing is the gang. Gang is more important than family, than school, than faith, than anything. It creates a sense of power and respect to be a gang member. These are often false feelings, but they are encouraged by the gang. Girls are groomed through gang indoctrination, which promotes the sense of identity and belonging. When they are "turned out," they are told to see it as a chore. It is their responsibility to help their family, their gang, and this is how they can do so. The impact of society is seen here, with the view that sex is "no big deal." They are told to view it as a way to earn money for something they have already been doing anyway. The gang tells them they are part of the family and that the gang wants them to succeed. In some cases, they have been told that the money they earn is being put in the bank for their college fund (Woolf, 2013).

Although for pimps the most important factor is to make money, gangs' primary consideration is not to get caught. Therefore, the methods through which they sell these girls differ from pimps. They tend to avoid Backpage because they know that law enforcement monitor it. They will only use it if they need a lot of money quickly. They are much more likely to use word of mouth or business cards in their own neighborhood. There is no electronic trail, and it is much harder to investigate (Woolf, 2013). Quotas are typically lower than those who are pimp controlled (McKeen & Blank, 2014).

Methods of selling will vary from gang to gang and area to area, but gangs will typically stay in their sphere of control in their neighborhood, using an apartment or having the girls go door to door. Clients must be trusted and pre-vetted. The gang is running countersurveillance, watching for cars or people that do not belong in their neighborhood. They are also able to offer lower prices than a pimp due to the number of girls. An average pimp will have two or three girls, while gangs typically have ten to twenty. However, Deepa Patel notes how much this changes, even moving from Northern Virginia to Washington, DC, as the area changes from suburban to urban. Territory possession is much stricter in the urban area, and girls may walk a track as compared to the suburban, wealthy area of Northern Virginia, where territory is more flexible and there is no track to walk, so girls may go door to door seeking buyers. The girls are monitored very closely and violence, in some cases extreme violence, is used to keep them in line (McKeen & Blank, 2014).

Identification and recovery of a person who has been trafficked by a gang can be even more complex than that of a person trafficked by a pimp. Although many law enforcement officers are now becoming aware that children who sell sex are crime victims, not crime perpetrators, in the case of those in a gang, they very frequently have committed other crimes that do squarely land them in violation of the law. Therefore, they are seen as a gang member, not a survivor of sex trafficking. Deepa Patel notes, "So that makes them a little bit different because a female that's out there beating other people up, they're not looked at as that victim, they're looked at as that criminal, that one that's aggressive engaging in these behaviors." They have been taught to see themselves in this way as well, further impeding investigation and recovery. The gang has indoctrinated them to feel that their primary loyalty is to the gang and not to their actual family. To limit identification by law enforcement or others, they may not have gang tattoos (McKeen & Blank, 2014).

For those who do think about leaving, gangs use the threat of their omnipresence of retribution for those who do want to leave or cooperate with law enforcement. Ms. Patel notes this as the biggest difference between pimp-controlled trafficking and gang-controlled trafficking, especially when it is an international gang, such as MS-13—the threat that they are everywhere and there is nowhere she can go that they will not find her. In 2003, an 18-year-old girl named Brenda Paz was killed after giving information to law enforcement about the activities of MS-13. She had been placed in protective custody and given a new identity, but she was pregnant, young, and isolated, and left the program. Three weeks after leaving, she was murdered and MS-13 is suspected in her death. Although this was one incident 10 years ago, it is still used by gangs to threaten those who may be considering leaving or cooperating with law enforcement.

The following case study illustrates one real-life example of gang trafficking that made national news, though of course, there are many other cases that do not.

_____

Justin Strom was a member of the Crips in Northern Virginia, who led a group trafficking girls in the region. Over a period of 6 years, girls were recruited online through Facebook, MySpace, and Datehookup. Strom used false profiles with female names to send hundreds of messages to lure girls in. They were also recruited in person at Metro stations, on the street, and in schools. They were told that they were pretty and could earn some money. Some were told initially it would only be dancing or stripping, or they were given some of the money initially. One 20-year-old woman, who was recruited when she was 16, stated that her parents had no idea; she would eat dinner and then sneak out at night.

They would then use the gang to bring them into sexual activity, giving the girls drugs and alcohol both as a reward and to ensure compliance. Violence, including rape, beatings, and chokings, was also

used to enforce compliance. The girls typically had to work most nights
and have sex with 5 to 10 men each night. They were taken door to
door and sold for 30 to 40 dollars for 15 minutes. They were also sold
online through Craigslist and Backpage.

The case was broken, thanks to an alert school attendance
officer who had been trained on this issue. This officer talked
with the girls, saw the red flags, and reported it. The ring was
broken through the joint efforts of the Fairfax County Police
department and the FBI. Strom was sentenced to 40 years for
his crimes; five other men were also sentenced. (case study
compiled from Jouvenal, 2012; U.S. Department of Justice, 2012;
Woolf, 2013)

Familial Trafficking

Little is written about familial trafficking, and it is often assessed as
child sexual abuse (Beck et al., 2015). A number of cases have made
the mass media, but often they are not referred to as trafficking. For example, a woman in Indiana was accused of selling her infant daughter
to a man for child pornography and convicted on charges related to
the production of child pornography ("Natisha Hilliard pleads guilty,"
2014). However, others are—one mother was convicted of human trafficking, among other charges, after a man had sex with her daughter
in "repayment" of $200 that he had lent her; her daughter was later
found raped and murdered ("Mother pleads guilty," 2013). In Utah, a
mother was convicted of sexual exploitation of a minor after attempting
to sell her 13-year-old daughter's virginity for $10,000 ("Mother who
tried," 2012).

Despite this confusion between trafficking and sex abuse, if the child is
traded for something of value, it is considered trafficking per the legal definition discussed in Chapter 1. Although trafficking by family members
does not receive a great deal of attention, one study in Kentucky found
that service providers reported that 82% of their three most recent trafficking survivors had been trafficked by a family member, as compared
to only 18% who identified an "intimate partner" as a trafficker (Cole &
Sprang, 2015). A study of youth served by Covenant House (2013)
in New York City found that of those who were trafficked, 36% were

trafficked by family members, as compared to 27% who reported being trafficked by a boyfriend.

Girls who were trafficked by family members have been found to be significantly younger when they first were trafficked than those trafficked by others (as young as 4 years old compared to 11 years old) and were significantly more likely to have witnessed domestic violence, experienced physical or sexual abuse, and experienced neglect or abandonment, as well as a combination of these types of maltreatment (Reid, Huard, & Haskell, 2015). The most common relative trafficker was the child's mother, and it was typically for financial gain. Reid et al. (2015) found that these mothers typically acted in one of three roles: madam (focused on arranging "dates" for money); addict (where the primarily purpose was to obtain drugs); or mentor (sought to train their daughter how to be a prostitute). In this study, of those trafficked by relatives, 37% (n=7) were trafficked by male relatives: cousins, uncles, and fathers.

Minh Dang is a survivor of trafficking by her parents and now uses her voice and experience to raise awareness of this aspect of trafficking.

Minh Dang was abused by her father from early childhood and she was 10 when her parents dropped her off at a brothel for the first time. They would leave her there for days or weeks at a time to earn money for them. She was still enrolled in school, earning high grades, and no one suspected what she was enduring. In college, Ms. Dang was able to break free and now uses her experience to help fight human trafficking. (summarized from Chan, 2013)

Ms. Dang notes that several components of the dynamics of control are similar to those of other forms of trafficking, but amplified because the trafficker is a family member. She states that children are vulnerable due to their dependency. Although pimps often make the youth feel dependent upon them, in the case of the family, this is exacerbated, because the child literally is dependent on them. They do not need to lie to the child to tell them that no one else will take care of them. Ms. Deng also notes the trafficked youth may feel ashamed and obliged to keep the secret of the trafficking. Although this is true in pimp-controlled trafficking, again, it is amplified by the cultural norm of keeping family problems private. Additionally, as with pimp-controlled trafficking, she states that those who are trafficked are often kept physically and/or emotionally i-solated. She also notes that incest can be a major component of family-controlled trafficking (Dang, as cited in Smith, 2014).

Survival Trafficking

When youth are on the street, they typically have no legal way to earn money for survival. They have not graduated high school, they have few job skills, they have no permanent residence, and depending on their age, they may not be legal to work. They may also lack government-issued proof of identification because they may be unable to obtain a driver's license or not have access to their Social Security card or birth certificate. Therefore, they must find another method of survival. Although it is this vulnerability that pimps exploit to lure in youth, youth may also be traf-ficked in other ways to meet their survival needs, such as by trading their body for survival needs, termed "survival sex." In these cases, the youth is not controlled by a pimp, but rather is brought into the trade by a friend or peer, perhaps a customer. The Trafficking Victims Protection Act (TVPA) does not require a third person to be in control of youth; these situations may fall under "obtaining or receipt," as detailed in the TVPA. Additionally, the TVPA states that trafficking includes the trading of sex for "anything of value." These items can include those needed for basic survival, such as food or shelter, or for other items, such as drugs. A study conducted by Covenant House (2013) in New York found that juveniles in their sample were equally likely to be considered trafficked due to force, fraud, or coercion (6.3% of the sample) as those who engaged in survival sex (5.7%).

In a study of youth arrested for prostitution, 23% of "solo operators" were boys as opposed to less than 1% of those exploited by a third party (Mitchell, Finkelhor, & Wolak, 2010). This was echoed in the study by Gwadz et al. (2009), who found that boys typically worked independ-ently, whereas girls were most commonly under the control of a pimp. About one third of their sample reported trading sex for money, food, shelter, or other compensation, with almost equal rates of boys and girls reporting this. As noted in Chapter 1, boys are less likely to see themselves as victims or may cast themselves as "hustlers" to denote more power in the situation. Dank (2011) found that boys were much more likely than either girls or transgendered youth to state they were brought into commercial sex by being approached by a customer (though this was still less common than a friend; 32% versus 44%). Lankenau et al. (2004) found that the boys stated they could often learn from other youth where the best spots to hustle were.

Although some buyers of these boys are female, the majority are men—primarily middle or upper class, White, professional, and married. The boys can be located on the street, on the Internet at such sites as Backpage.com or rentboy.com, in clubs and bars, and a number of other places. Among homeless youth, those who identify as gay, lesbian, or bisexual are more significantly more likely to engage in survival sex than heterosexual youth (Gangamma, Slesnick, Toviessi, & Serovich, 2008). However, many of these boys are heterosexual; as one youth stated, "I don't consider myself homosexual at all. I just gotta do what I gotta do and so I can eat every day. I don't like the fact that I have to be with another man just to survive" (Dank, 2011, p. 101). This is sometimes termed "gay for pay." This engagement in sex with a man in order to meet one's needs inhibits identification as someone who has been trafficked, both self-identification and identification by professionals. These boys frequently do not want to admit their engagement in these acts due to the stigma associated with homosexuality, whereas professionals do not see the boys as exploited.

Transgendered youth are much more likely to state that they were brought into commercial sex by friends than cisgender youth (Dank, 2011). One study of trans* female-identified youth ages 15 to 24 years found that two thirds had engaged in sex work, either for money or food/shelter. For those who were under 18 years old at the time, this is trafficking. The authors found that those who perceived *more* social support from their family of choice were more likely to engage in sex work (Wilson et al., 2009). This may be because this group of youth is more likely to work together in a more equal situation, noting it is their "family of choice," not family of origin. Rather than being "controlled" by a pimp, the dynamics are often different for them.

Tina Frundt, executive director of Courtney's House in Washington, DC, notes that half of her clients are boys, who often are brought into the life by a buyer. The buyer may bring the boy to his house and then have a trafficker come there. In other cases, the buyer drops the boy off on the track, where they are promptly recruited. For trans* youth, the dynamics of control are different than they are for girls who are controlled by a pimp. The group is often headed by a "mama," who is a transwoman and who also works in the sex trade. The group lives together in a house and operates more as a "family." It may be the first time the youth has felt accepted in their full identity, and it may be their "family of choice."

Those engaged in survival sex can be among the most difficult to identify because they are not controlled by a third party. They see themselves as empowered and doing what they must to survive. For those who believe that trafficking requires a third party who controls the youth, they will not consider these children to be trafficked. However, the buyers of these children are engaged in a crime, and these youth should not have to trade their bodies to meet their needs.

As noted, these are the four primary currently known methods of how children are bought and sold for sex in the United States: pimp controlled, gang controlled, familial, and survival. It is expected that as awareness of this crime grows, these methods will continue to evolve. However, this chapter provides a basic current understanding of trafficking situations.

Conclusion

Throughout this chapter, we have seen that these youth can be both difficult to identify and to assist in exiting the life. Thus, the next chapter will focus on how this can be done.

3

Exiting the Life

As discussed in Chapter 2, survivors of sex trafficking can be difficult to identify and assist. This is due not only to difficulties in self-identification or coaching by traffickers but also to lack of understanding on the part of those in society responsible for assisting them, including law enforcement, medical personnel, and social service providers. Youth often do not self-identify as needing assistance for a variety of reasons. Many do not know what human trafficking is and thus cannot identify themselves as victims of it. As noted in Chapter 1, this can be especially true for boys, who are socialized not to see themselves as victims, but as active agents, viewing themselves as "hustlers" rather than trafficked. For those who were maltreated previously, they may not know that life can be another way (West & Loeffler, 2015). Because they are still children, they will typically lack the emotional maturity to process the situation they are in and develop options (West & Loeffler, 2015).

The trafficker may also use violence or the threat of violence to keep them from seeking assistance should they start to consider it. These children can be moved from place to place to prevent them from forming any bonds to anyone who might help them. Youth often fear returning home, perhaps because they have fled an abusive situation or because they fear telling their family what has happened to them. They are ashamed of what they have done, and the trafficker has often told them no one will want them because of the stigma attached to being a "whore." Many have been led to believe by their trafficker that the situation they are in is of their own making and therefore there is nothing they can do to get out.

Smith (2014, p. 107) states of her experience, "I believed I had brought all this on myself. Because I had chosen to run away with this man. I believed that I deserved what was happening to me." Because the youth believes this is a path they have chosen and the only option they have open to them, they often have a bad attitude toward law enforcement and others they see as "squares," who cannot understand their world. They have become used to having to manipulate people in order to have their needs met and will carry those survival skills with them, even once out of the life. They believe (often correctly) that providers cannot handle the full truth of their experiences and thus will never fully trust them. As discussed in Chapter 4 on services, helping survivors to recover from their experiences is very difficult, complex work that requires a well-developed set of professional skills.

For those who have a third-party exploiter, they have been coached on how to handle the situation, including lying about their age and the fact that they are working for someone, as well as being given fake IDs. Corporal Chris Heid of the Maryland State Police notes, "From what the girls are telling us—everyone will tell us they had a pimp, but nobody will say 'I have a pimp.'" These exploiters have psychologically trained the youth that they are the only ones who truly care about them and thus the youth go along with this. They use the bond with the child described in the previous chapter to keep the child from leaving (West & Loeffler, 2015).

For those survivors who have been previously involved in a system, whether it be child welfare or juvenile justice, they often have already experienced disinterest on the part of adults to help them as youth feel they need and thus it is all too easy for them to believe that no one is interested in helping them. They have been told that law enforcement will arrest them for prostitution and they cannot expect any help from officers. They will likely have seen others arrested or have been arrested themselves for prostitution, validating what they are told. For example, a study in Kentucky with service providers found that half of the survivors with whom they interacted had been charged with a criminal offense (Cole & Anderson, 2013).

These youth often are correct that they will be judged. As discussed, the media image that many people identify with the sex trafficking of minors is a White suburban girl who is kidnapped and chained to a radiator. This leads to the idea of a grateful child who will heap praise upon those who "rescue" her. However, as detailed in this book, the reality is typically far different. Rather than being kidnapped and physically restrained, most are caught in a web of psychological coercion and a drive to survive. Although it can appear from the outside that they could leave at any time, this is usually not the case. Especially for the majority of survivors who are not physically restrained, judgments about their ability to leave the situation can cast them as a "bad victim." Those who work with survivors have stated that these social judgments of "good victims" and "bad victims" affect survivors' willingness to be identified and to receive services (West & Loeffler, 2015).

The Trafficking Victims Protection Act clearly outlines that any youth under 18 years of age who is selling sex acts in any fashion is trafficked—children cannot consent to selling themselves. However, the idea of a "child prostitute" still lingers in many minds. Shared Hope International (2014) discusses a case in which a boy was reported to the police by a friend who saw him advertised online. The police gained access to his e-mail and found detailed e-mails with one buyer and identified another possible buyer. However, the boy did not want to press charges, and the police declined to continue the case because they believed the boy was advertising himself, reflecting a lack of knowledge of what constitutes sex trafficking of a child. Law enforcement may see the youth as criminals, rather than crime victims, and arrest them on prostitution charges. This can especially be true for those engaged in survival sex because they do not fit the media image of a trafficking survivor.

When law enforcement encounter a situation in which a youth is selling sex, several factors affect whether that youth is seen as a crime victim or a crime perpetrator. Girls are more likely to be seen as victims, as are those being exploited by a third party (e.g., a pimp). If the case came to the attention of police by a report, as opposed to a police action such as a raid, this makes it more likely that the youth will be seen as a victim. Children who are younger, have a history of running away, or are seen as frightened, dirty, or have body odor are all more likely to be perceived as crime victims (Mitchell, Finkelhor, & Wolak, 2010).

Whether or not the case involved the use of the Internet is also a significant factor. One study found that cases that did involve the Internet were more likely to have the youth treated as a crime victim than a delinquent: 91% of cases as opposed to 61% of cases that did not involve the Internet. These cases were also significantly more likely to involve younger girls and a third-party exploiter (pimp or family member) than cases that did not (Wells, Mitchell, & Ji, 2012). Police may also assess the youth into other categories if they are not familiar with the nuances of trafficking. Special Agent Louis Morlier, a federal criminal investigator with the Department of Homeland Security, notes that:

Police are more likely, at least now, to view these youth as an offender, what they tend to call a delinquent youth or a runaway. Someone who is committing a status offense. When they encounter a minor and they say, "Where are your parents?" and they either give a false answer or that they don't know, the officer runs that child in a law enforcement database and finds out that they've run away from the neighboring state. As soon as they hear the word "runaway," it triggers a response, and the idea that maybe this is a victim of minor trafficking is forgotten.

Identification of Survivors

Locating missing youth is an essential first step to preventing or recovering youth who may be trafficked. The National Center for Missing and Exploited Children (NCMEC) has two primary methods by which they receive reports of missing and exploited children. Authorized to serve as the nation's clearinghouse on these issues, NCMEC operates a hotline, 1-800-THE-LOST® (1-800-843-5678), and has assisted law enforcement in the recovery of more than 208,500 children. The NCMEC also operates the CyberTipline®, a mechanism for reporting child pornography, child sex trafficking, and other forms of child sexual exploitation. Since the CyberTipline launched in 1998, more than 4.9 million reports of suspected child sexual exploitation have been received. The NCMEC receives grant funding from the US Department of Justice's Office of Juvenile Justice and Delinquency Prevention for many of these programs.

Only paid staff who have undergone 3 months of training answer the phone to ensure that each call is well handled and the needed information is gathered, to the extent possible. Although they rely on the information provided, the caller may not be aware of the signs of exploitation and therefore be unable to report it as a risk. Therefore, the NCMEC has been working on internal systems to better identify children who are reported as missing who may also be being exploited. Indicators include the risk factors discussed in Chapter 1, including gang involvement, a history of exploitation, sexual abuse, and homelessness.

Melissa Snow, the program specialist on child sex trafficking, helps to "connect the dots" on indicators of potential exploitation, so when missing children are reported, the reporter does not need to be aware of these indicators or name exploitation, but NCMEC can assist in the identification of the cases and assign them to team members who specialize in case management and outreach for this population. If the child has run before, the specialized case management and analytical teams are able to access all of the previous times the child was listed as missing with NCMEC and all the information it contains. This can be particularly helpful if a new law enforcement officer or social worker has been assigned to the case and may not have access to that historical information. NCMEC also receives thousands of reports every month through the CyberTipline of potential exploitation of children through online classified ads. The Child Sex Trafficking Team analysts will look at those listed in online classified ads and cross-check them with children reported missing to help locate and name exploited children.

Signs of Trafficking

Because youth are unlikely to self-identify, it is important that adults who interact with them are trained in how to do so. This can include professionals such as law enforcement, medical personnel, and social service staff but also those in other industries who may interact with them such as school staff, those working at hotels, and truckers. However, as noted, this requires these professionals to discard outdated images of "child prostitutes" and what a trafficked person looks like.

Depending on the situation in which one encounters the youth, signs of trafficking may vary. A person who knows them in school, such as a school nurse, a teacher, or a friend, may see changes that can indicate a trafficking situation. On the other hand, someone encountering them for the first time, such as law enforcement or emergency room personnel, would note different signs. Box 3.1 summarizes signs of potential DMST that have been gathered from various sources, including Goldblatt Grace, Starck, Potenza, Kenney, & Sheetz (2012). They center on signs of pimp-controlled trafficking, because this is the type about which most is known, but could signal other types as well. Additionally, although these

BOX 3.1 Signs of Domestic Minor Sex Trafficking

- Excess amount of cash
- Hotel room keys
- Lying about age/false identification
- Inconsistencies in story
- Lack of knowledge of a given community or whereabouts
- Inability or fear to make eye contact
- Restricted/scripted communication
- Claims of being an adult, although appearance suggests adolescent features
- Visible signs of abuse, including unexplained bruises, black eyes, cuts, or marks. Often marks or bruising in discreet areas (i.e., not on face) in order to preserve appearance for marketability.
- Behaviors consistent with post-traumatic stress disorder, such as fear, anxiety, or hypervigilance
- A history of childhood sexual abuse/incest, physical abuse/neglect, and/or sexual assault
- A history of running away and/or multiple unexplained absences from school
- Changes in physical appearance, including but not limited to:
  - new expensive clothes or accessories;
  - expensive hairdos and nails;
  - sexually suggestive clothes or makeup; and/or
  - frequent changes in the color or style of hair.
- A tattoo that the child is reluctant to explain
- A facial scar, which, like tattoos, is used to brand the child as a property of a particular owner
- Exhaustion
- Multiple cell phones
- Feeling that she or he must check a cell phone immediately
- Language from "the life," such as a girl referring to her boyfriend as "daddy" or using a street name
- Involvement with a male who has one or more of the following characteristics:
  - He is older
  - He goes by a street name (i.e., Zeus, Too Sweet, etc.), and the child is not aware of his real name
  - He always has a lot of money, but the child does not know how he makes a living
  - He is violent and controlling toward the child
  - He buys the child a cell phone
- A history of multiple sexually transmitted infections and/or pregnancies. The child may seek regular testing for HIV
- An inordinate amount of time spent online, including the following behaviors:
  - A sexually explicit online profile on Black Planet, MySpace, Facebook, or other Internet sites
  - Frequents Internet chat rooms or classified sites, such as Backpage
- An interest in pornography or other aspects of the sex industry
- New friends, including those who are much older

(continued)

- Disconnection from family or other caregivers
- Complaints by teachers of inappropriate behaviors in the classroom, including passing of notes with sexually explicitly statements and an inability to focus on academics while often appearing confused
- Expressions of suicidal ideation or use of cutting as a coping skill
- Exchange of money with other students while passing in the corridor
- Talk among other students, some becoming fearful while others are disgusted
- Poor supervision at home, failure to go home after school, and lack of parent awareness of where the child is or with whom after school
- Frequent sleepovers with "friends"

are standardized signs, there may be others that signal something unusual is occurring. Tina Frundt of Courtney's House notes that, as a survivor, she knows some of those odd signs, such as using makeup sponges during the menstrual cycle rather than a tampon since she was forced to work during her period (Westerman, 2014). Additionally, while one of these signs on its own would not necessarily indicate trafficking, several of them together should raise concern.

Law Enforcement

Law enforcement officers, often the first to encounter a survivor, face a particularly tough battle. Survivors have likely seen their friends arrested and may have been arrested themselves. The trafficker has told them that no one else cares about them and that cops only want to arrest them. Therefore, law enforcement officers need to work with these individuals in ways that are different from other victims of crime. It may not be the first time that law enforcement talks with them that they will tell the officer what is going on, and it may not be the fifth time, but the officers must be patient and understanding, as each time may be the critical time.

A variety of law enforcement officers and agencies may encounter a survivor of trafficking or uncover trafficking in the course of their duties. Local law enforcement are the most likely to come across this crime due to their intimate knowledge of their jurisdiction. For those who are trafficked in multiple cities, law enforcement officers may encounter them while they are in transport, such as at gas stations, truck stops, and hotels (Bales & Lize, 2005). For those trafficked in one place, they may be found on the street, or also in truck stops and hotels. However, lack of training for officers means they are not always aware that they are interacting with a trafficking survivor (Farrell, McDevitt, & Fahy, 2008; Irazola, Williamson, Chen, Garrett, & Clawson 2008; Renzetti, Bush, Castellanos, & Hunt, 2015), and thus they do not necessarily take immediate action or assess the situation accurately (Bales & Lize, 2005). Existing studies suggest that few officers receive training regarding human trafficking (Farrell, 2012; Farrell, McDevitt, & Fahy, 2010; Farrell & Pfeffer, 2014; Grubb & Bennett, 2012), and a lack of training limits their ability to identify and respond to cases of trafficking (Farrell, Pfeffer, & Bright, 2015).

Federal law enforcement may also work with survivors of this crime. Immigration and Customs Enforcement of the Department of Homeland Security also work these cases because anything related to the Internet or use of cell phones is considered to have crossed national borders, thus involving Customs. State troopers may come across this in the course of their normal duties as well. Corporal Chris Heid of the Maryland State Police now works in a specialized unit that focuses on recovering missing children, especially those who have been trafficked. Reflecting back on his previous assignment patrolling, he thinks that in some of the traffic stops he made, there might have been human trafficking occurring, but at that time he did not know what human trafficking was or what to look for. He thinks training would make a big difference for officers to have them assess for human trafficking as well as drug trafficking:

If you make a traffic stop on I-95 and you get a guy and girl coming from Florida or North Carolina up here, I think a police officer's main focus used to be, "Well, I wonder if they're involved in drugs." I think we should get, and I think we are getting, more training, but if we could get everybody trained to not only looking for drugs, but also looking for human trafficking. When you say, "What is human trafficking?" to a police officer, myself included previously, it was, "Oh that's bringing in a girl up from Mexico and making her a prostitute or work for you" . . . . Everybody knows what prostitution is, but I don't think everybody knows what human trafficking is.

The reaction of law enforcement officers, often the first professionals to encounter youth who are being trafficked, is critical. If youth feel judged, they will immediately shut down. Due to the lies they have been told by their trafficker or previous negative encounters, they are unlikely to perceive the officer as a source of assistance. Therefore, they often appear as having a "bad attitude" and not wanting assistance. It is critical that the officer remember the psychological manipulation the youth is likely to have experienced and not to take anything personally. Smith (2014) notes the bad experience she had when recovered by law enforcement and that "without immediate support and understanding from law enforcement, child victims of sex trafficking are left only with the support and understanding offered by their traffickers" (p. 128). She then goes on to note how she had been "handled" by six different officers due to the variety of jurisdictions, and that she was interviewed as though she were an adult, not the 14-year-old child in crisis that she was. The relentless questioning left her feeling "ashamed, humiliated and exposed," and resulted in her trying to hold back as much information as possible (p. 133).

The National Criminal Justice Training Center's course on how to interview a child who potentially has been sexually exploited is 3 full days—just on the interview techniques alone. The overview course is another 3 days. This emphasizes the intricacy and delicateness that must be used when working with those who have been trafficked. For example, if youth are brought to a police station, they should never be asked to wait in a cell, but rather a waiting room or lobby.

The Dallas Police Department has been recognized for leading the way in survivor-centered response. Sergeant Byron Fassett and Detective Catherine De La Paz developed a High-Risk Victims and Trafficking Team as they came to realize that the youth were not choosing to be involved in prostitution, but rather were manipulated or felt they had no other options (Smith, 2014). Started in 2005, this model is survivor centered and multidisciplinary. High-risk victims are identified as those who have multiple runaway episodes, run away before they are 12 years old, have been sexually exploited while running away, have been repeatedly sexually abused or exploited, and/or have been trafficked (Fassett, 2012; Smith, 2014).

Any youth identified as being a high-risk victim is referred to the team—24 hours a day, 7 days a week. The team has developed a specific interview and assessment model to work with survivors as they recognize that traditional methods of policing are ineffective with this population. The model is based on the recognition that trust must be developed between the youth and the team, and this will take time and multiple meetings to develop (Smith, 2014).

In Chicago, police have also adapted their methods to better address issues related to trafficking. The Child Protection Response Unit was developed in Cook County to take a more proactive response to locating youth who go missing from the child welfare system, recognizing them as high risk for being trafficked or involved in crime. Previously, it may have taken days for these children to be registered as missing, and sometimes little effort was put forth to locate them. Now, the team meets each morning to review the list of those missing and to work on locating them (Smith, M., 2015).

The Maryland State Police has developed a Child Recovery Unit to assist in locating missing children, including those who may be trafficked. Corporal Chris Heid looks for indicators such as running from foster care, being an adolescent, or having their Facebook photos taken in a hotel room. They will then look online at sites such as Backpage to see if they can identify the youth. If he locates her (they have mostly worked with girls), he will make a date over the phone, but as soon as he shows up at the door, he identifies himself as a police officer. He is typically accompanied by his Sergeant, who is female. They will talk with the girl, usually for about an hour, to let her know her options and to give her referrals to local organizations, such as TurnAround in Baltimore. They dress very casually and work to develop a rapport with the girl so she feels comfortable. They emphasize that they will never force her to do anything. He often stays in touch with the girls for long periods of time, and they like to contact him to let him know how well they are doing after leaving the life, illustrating the quality of the rapport they develop.

Corporal Heid notes several indicators of success of their approach. The first indicator is the number of girls who choose to come with them or to take the referral. Second, even if the girl does not choose to come with them, they rarely see a repeat. Lastly, pimps have told him that they know about his team and avoid working with juveniles because of it. He states that an admitted pimp told him, "I've heard about you guys. I can get in a lot of trouble if we had a juvenile, so I make everybody show me their ID." Corporal Heid regards this as a major validation of the impact of their team.

Thus, training is essential for all officers as they may come across those who have been trafficked in the course of their normal duties. In addition, specialized units should be created to address the nuances related to this crime—locating and recovering those at risk for or currently trafficked. However, only 29 states now have laws that encourage or mandate law enforcement training (Polaris, 2015a), and these types of teams are still rare.

Social Service Providers

Children who are at risk for, or are being trafficked, are frequently in contact with service providers, whether that is in school or in the community. Youth who are in foster care, have run away, struggle with mental health issues, are living in poverty, or are members of a sexual minority may well already be receiving services. However, as noted, all types of children have been trafficked, and not being an identified member of one of these groups does not mean a child is immune from trafficking. Thus, *all* professionals who work with youth should be aware of the basic facts of sex trafficking and signs that a youth may exhibit. Having a standard screening for those at medical facilities or social service agencies facilitates identification. However, currently this is not common. One study in Kentucky found that three quarters of surveyed professionals working with at-risk youth or crime victims stated that their agencies did not have a protocol for screening for trafficking. Despite this, half had worked with a confirmed or suspected survivor of trafficking (Cole & Anderson, 2013). Vera Institute has developed a screening tool that is available on its website that can help identify those who have been trafficked, domestic or foreign, for either labor or sexual exploitation (www.vera.org), as has Shared Hope International in their publication *Intervene* (Leitch & Snow, 2013).

When youth run away and then return home, they often do not discuss where they have been or what happened while they were gone. Youth may be too embarrassed or scared to discuss what happened, and if they are involved with the foster care or juvenile justice system, those system workers are often focused on where to place them now that they have returned rather than on what happened while they were gone. Therefore, Amelia Rubenstein, MSW of TurnAround in Baltimore, Maryland, developed a screening tool to help flag youth who may have been sexually exploited.

One key factor is runaway history: assessing how often the youth have run, how long they were gone, and how far they went. She notes that a youth who ran for 12 hours and says she went to a friend's house is very different than one who was gone for 3 months and says she was in Atlantic City. To find out this information in a nonthreatening way, she will ask them where they spent the previous night, as that appears to be an innocuous question. If they say a hotel room, that is a red flag, since most youth cannot rent a room on their own, never mind afford it. She also assesses what the youth is carrying when they return: hotel keys, prepaid credit cards, large amounts of cash, expensive electronics, or certain brands of condoms in large quantities can all be indicators. Tattoos can also be another sign.

Probation officers should also be screening the youth on their caseloads for sexual exploitation. Especially in the case of gang-controlled trafficking, the youth may be arrested for other crimes but may be being trafficked. Tesy Molina, who works with survivors of gang trafficking, notes that youth may be picked up by police at a hotel at midnight and brought home, but no one asks why they were there; they are just scolded by their probation officer for being out past curfew. The unasked question leaves that youth still exploited

Health Care Providers

Health care providers are an essential resource in identifying those who are being trafficked. Emergency room providers may see those who are currently exploited being brought in for injuries. Clinics, including urgent care clinics and reproductive health care clinics, may see others with non-emergency needs. School nurses are another vital resource. If protocols are developed and assessment methods taught, as has been done for domestic violence, this can help identify survivors at an earlier point than currently exists. However, similar to other professionals, lack of training and awareness of trafficking has been found to be a barrier in accurate identification of trafficking in professionals in hospitals and clinics (Beck et al., 2015). Information has been published for school nurses on how to identify children at their schools who are being trafficked (Goldblatt Grace, et al., 2012). For all health care providers, indicators may include the following:

• The person is accompanied by a domineering adult.
• The person is not allowed to be alone.
• The person is not allowed to speak for himself or herself.

- There are suspicious injuries.
- The information the person gives regarding demographics changes.
- The person has multiple sexually transmitted infections (STIs).
- The person reports having more than two sexual partners.
- The person reports more than 10 sexual partners over his or her lifetime. (Compiled from Chang, Lee, Park, Sy, & Quach, 2015; Greenbaum, Crawford-Jakubiak and the Committee on Child Abuse and Neglect, 2015; Hom & Woods, 2013)

Greenbaum et al. (2015) also offer specific follow-up questions that the health care providers can ask to determine if the child is being trafficked, as well as detailed suggestions for how to conduct the assessment. Even if the youth is with a person who seems trustworthy, such as a parent, police officer, or social worker, the medical provider should still speak with them alone because the youth may be too embarrassed to discuss the situation in front of them or feel they will not understand. Medical providers should also remember that a parent can be a trafficker.

Just as when working with victims of other types of crime, sensitivity and understanding are essential, as is use of judgment on how to proceed. As noted previously, many of these girls may not view themselves as exploited. Even if they do, they may not feel able to leave the trafficking situation. The provider must accept this if it arises but provide them with resources for further support for when they do feel ready (Hom & Woods, 2013).

Truckers

As noted in Chapter 2, truckers have long been a target for those selling sexual services. When they park at a truck stop for the night, they are often solicited, or they may receive solicitations over the CB radio. Therefore, truckers are quite likely to encounter those who have been trafficked, including trafficked youth. Truckers Against Trafficking has been working to educate their fellow truckers about the issue and what to do if they encounter a situation that they believe could be trafficking. Truckers are ideal assistants because they can typically report a potential case while the person is still in sight and law enforcement can make an immediate response.

Leaving the Life

It is not enough to simply identify those who are being trafficked; we must help them to leave the situation. As has been discussed throughout this book, this is not a simple process, due to the complexity of the situation, and it will vary by type of trafficking as well as by each person's unique circumstances. For many survivors, this can be a lengthy process, and it may require multiple contacts, but each person should approach it with hope as this may be the exact time the trafficked youth feels able to leave.

For those involved in gang-controlled trafficking, the story of Brenda Paz, which is discussed in Chapter 2, is used as a constant threat for those who want to leave before the gang is finished with them. Those who are trafficked by a family member may be completely dependent on that person for their survival and have very complex psychological bonds to them as a family member, especially a mother. For those who are pimp controlled, they likely fear the violence that will likely result if they try to leave (Williamson & Cluse-Tolar, 2002). They may be constantly monitored to ensure they are obeying the rules (Nixon et al., 2002). Even if there is not someone physically with them, they may need to be accessible by phone or report in at a particular time. They may feel psychological ties to their trafficker and love him or her (Williamson & Cluse-Tolar, 2002). They also believe they have brought this situation on themselves due to bad choices or not following the established rules and thus blame themselves for the situation (Williamson & Cluse-Tolar, 2002). Even for those who are comparatively free to leave, the need for the money can be hard to meet elsewhere. They may need this money for survival needs, including food and shelter, or for a drug addiction. For some, they have been doing it for so long, it has become part of their identity (Nixon et al., 2002). They may feel that they are not good enough for anything else or know how to exit.

Donna Gavin, lieutenant in the Boston Police Department and the commander of the Human Trafficking Unit, notes that pimps will tell youth, "You got nothing, nobody cares about you, you're just a whore, that's all you are. Cops aren't gonna believe you," to prevent them from seeking help. She also states that some trafficked youth are forced into doing other crimes to make their quota, like credit cards, fraud, or stealing, which also inhibits them from seeking assistance.

Due to previous bad experiences with the police or service providers, including violence or arrest, they may not be willing to approach law enforcement for assistance. They may also have asked for assistance in the past from police and not been taken seriously (Williamson & Cluse-Tolar, 2002). Police may believe the lines she has been taught to say—that she is independent, that she is a high-class call girl, that she lives well. However, investigation often shows that while a girl may project this image, she is actually living on a mattress in a dirty, cockroach-infested apartment while her pimp pockets all the money.

One study of sexually exploited girls solicited advice from them on effective street outreach techniques (Holger-Ambrose, Langmade, Edinburgh, & Saewyc, 2013). The girls stated they thought the following tips were important for outreach workers:

- Be real and respectful.
- Build up trust.
- Be brief and do not push yourselves on people.
- Provide youth with resources.
- Be nonjudgmental.
- Listen.
- Be in a place without bars on the windows.
- Care.

Girls noted they wanted workers to use "soft words," meaning that the clinical or legal terms used by professionals should be avoided and gentler words used in their place. They also noted that they would like workers to carry supplies, including condoms, lubricant, and hygiene supplies. A number of them stated they would like them to have information about service providers that they could give out.

As discussed, Corporal Heid of the Maryland State Police works hard to help the girls he locates feel comfortable and not judged. He and his female partner are dressed in everyday clothes, such as jeans and a sweatshirt, in order to make girls comfortable and to establish a rapport where they can talk in a relaxed manner with each other:

I think it's a different perspective than a guy walking in with a shirt and tie on, and clean-shaven. I think we come down to their level, we sit on the bed with them, or sit on the dresser across from them and we just talk. We're not asking a lot of direct questions. Yeah, we do want to know, and we'll ask, "Is there any chance anybody is watching right now, because I don't want to put you in the middle of anything. Tell me, if you don't want to talk, that's fine, but we need to talk to something because I don't want you going out of here, or us leaving here and somebody comes back and you get beaten because the police were here."

———————

They will talk with girls about their options and offer to connect them to social services. In the Baltimore area, they primarily connect with TurnAround, but there are other agencies able to offer support depending on the location. He states, "Our focus is not to make a case; our focus is to get that girl out of the situation she's in at that current time. If we can make a case, great, but if we can get her out, that's better."

Once they connect the girls with social services, depending on the agency, the providers may be leery of law enforcement and their desire to stay connected, as some law enforcement officers can be focused on making the "case" at the expense of the survivors and regardless of their desires. Farrell and Pfeffer (2014) note that lack of a cooperative relationship between law enforcement and social service providers can leave the survivors caught in between: Service providers may refrain from referring cases to law enforcement so that survivors are not arrested, and law enforcement feels that while an arrest can harm the relationship, without access to survivors, they need to arrest them to gain access and ensure the trafficking ceases.

Corporal Heid is very upfront about not pushing any survivor into more than she wants; Heid wants to let the girl know they care about her as a person, not as a case. He states, "We just stop by to take her to lunch. Say hey, we're still involved in your life if you want us to be. If not, that's fine, but we try more to build relationships with these girls." But some staff members are leery of law enforcement and question his motives, perhaps due to previous poor interactions with the legal system. They will question them, "What are you really up to?" He tells them, "What we're up to is we wanted to bring her something to eat. And I'm sure they thought with that in the past, with law enforcement that 'Well, they're going to say they want this, but when they get there, they're going to question her about that'—I told them, 'You're more than welcome to come along, but I'm not buying you lunch.'"

Conclusion

As discussed, identifying survivors and assisting them in feeling able to leave their situation can be an intricate and delicate process. Once successful, though, it is essential to connect survivors to appropriate services and to help them heal from the trafficking and to give them the skills to successfully move on in their lives. This can be an even more intricate and delicate process. Although many agencies are popping up to offer services, assisting someone in healing from complex trauma is advanced clinical work that requires a high level of skill, as will be discussed in Chapter 4.

4

Impacts of Trafficking and Services to Address Them

Being trafficked can result in a broad variety of impacts on the survivor—physical, psychological, and social—and often requires professional assistance to overcome. Physical health concerns, including reproductive health issues, are common. Addictions may also be present because substance use is a common coping mechanism for survivors. Social issues, including difficulties in trust, being behind in school, and needing job skills, can also serve as barriers to reintegrating into everyday life. Case management may be needed to connect survivors to appropriate resources, and survivors may lack life skills, such as how to pay bills, manage a checking account, or apply for a job. Clinicians with advanced training and a clear understanding of the dynamics of trafficking and trauma are required to help heal the psychological and social impacts, which have often compounded earlier childhood traumas As noted by Julie Laurence, chief program officer at GEMS in New York City, healing is a long journey. She states:

_____

It's really about providing support for the crisis, the day-to-day urgent needs the girls have, but then encompassing that into a really long-term holistic approach. It's not just getting someone out of a bad situation at 3 in the morning; we do that, but that's a short-term thing. It's really about providing an ongoing community of support and healing that we have found is most effective. Some people focus on "rescuing" them and blaming bad men and poor little girls and trying to take girls out of the situation and putting them somewhere in a house for 6 months and everything should be fine. That sort of short-term approach doesn't work. If you just do that without doing the other long-term work that's needed, that can be a little bit dangerous.

Physical Impacts

Physical injuries resulting from violence are common for trafficking survivors because those who are sold for sex experience a high level of violence in the course of their work. Farley et al. (2003), in their sample that included men, women, girls, and transgendered persons in the United States, found that while being prostituted, 82% had been physically assaulted, 73% had been raped, and of those raped, 60% had been raped more than five times. Ninety-five percent reported that 1½ years after leaving prostitution, they were still suffering from an injury received as a result of violence. The same percentage cited suffering from a head injury, and 72% noted memory problems.

In Chapter 2, it was described how many girls reported experiencing a high level of violence from their pimps. While this is true, it is important to note that many also experience violence at the hands of buyers. One study of adult women found that 8.5% had been raped by their pimp and 26.2% reported assault, while in contrast, 42.7% reported being raped by a buyer with 54.8% experiencing assault at the hands of a buyer (Clarke, Clarke, Roe-Sepowitz, & Fey, 2012). Murder is not uncommon, while stabbings, gang rapes, kidnappings, being hit by a car, and torture also occur. One formerly exploited woman stated the following about buyers:

The Johns, you know the buyers, they don't buy people to treat them well. So every act is usually a form of either a rougher than normal act or a deviant act. So the amount of health issues are truly endless. (Hom & Woods, 2013, p. 77)

Sexually transmitted diseases, including HIV/AIDS, are another common issue with which survivors may need to cope (Clawson & Goldblatt Grace, 2007; Macias-Konstantopoulos et al., 2015; Nixon et al., 2002). Female survivors may also be pregnant, have difficulties relating to fertility, or other gynecological issues (Clawson & Goldblatt Grace, 2007; Irazola, Wlliamson, Chen, Garrett, & Clawson, 2008; Macias-Konstantopoulos et al., 2015). Additionally, survivors may have dental issues (Irazola et al., 2008).

The hyperarousal experienced during trafficking can lead to an increased risk for substance abuse due to difficulties in moderating the biological stress. Bonnie Martin, a therapist in Alexandria, Virginia, who has been working with survivors of trafficking for 15 years, notes that many of her clients who have been trafficked struggle with substance abuse issues. She notes that a huge gap in the treatment field is a lack of integration of traumatic stress treatment and substance abuse treatment. While some enter the life to be able to access drugs, others use substances as a method of coping. Survivors may have difficulties in calming themselves from arousal, including being able to go to sleep. They may also have difficulties dealing with "too much calm" and may use drugs or alcohol to moderate that stress or to cope with disassociation.

Drugs and alcohol may also have been used by the survivor while being trafficked to ease the sex act. Kramer (2003) in her sample of adults found that 70% reported using drugs or alcohol in order to be able to detach emotionally during the sex act; 54% said this was necessary in order to be able to complete the act, and 45% said they needed it to cope with fear. Crack cocaine or methamphetamines are often used as stimulants, whereas benzodiazepines such as klonopin are used as numbing agents. Traffickers often use substances to either elicit sexual excitement or to numb the child to the sex act that is occurring. Addiction can also be used to bind them to the trafficker in order to obtain the drugs.

Physical health issues resulting from trafficking may not show up right away, in fact, perhaps not for years. Research has found that trauma experienced as a child can result in long-term physical problems. Though research on the impact of trafficking is too new to assess its long-term impacts, lessons can be learned from other studies. The multitude of studies assessing adverse childhood experiences (ACEs) have found that traumatic experiences as a child, including maltreatment and household dysfunction, can result in a myriad of long-term health problems as an adult, including higher rates of heart and liver disease (Centers for Disease Control, 2014). Those who are diagnosed with post-traumatic stress disorder (PTSD) have been found to have higher rates of back pain, hypertension, cancer, strokes, and digestive disorders among many others (summarized in Briere & Scott 2013). Thus, those trafficked as children may have physical health problems that do not emerge for decades but will have their roots in the experience of being trafficked.

Impact on the Brain

As discussed in Chapter 1, trauma also takes its toll on the brain, thus creating a bridge between physical impacts and psychological impacts. Understanding the impact of trauma on the brain is essential to understanding how to assist survivors. Bonnie Martin states:

For these clients particularly, when they finally make it into treatment, they have so many different diagnoses: ADHD, conduct disorder, sexual disorders, eating disorders, anxiety, depression, etc. The clinician is trained to provide evidence-based treatment for a certain diagnosis. What is usually at the root of these diagnoses, maladaptive coping mechanisms and behavioral issues, is trauma, particularly complex trauma, trauma that is interpersonal and violent. And so instead of treatment being driven by many different evidence-based models for the different diagnoses, it should be driven by our understanding of the biological reaction of stress in the brain and body, and how identity forms and attachment styles are impacted by repeated traumatic stress.

She bases her approach on the work of Dr. John Arden's brain-based therapy model. As explained in Arden and Linford (2009), this approach works from a BASE: B—Brain-based; A—Attunement; S—Systems; E—Evidence-based practice. Arden and Linford (2009) note that as more is learned about how the brain functions, it is drawing together what we have considered the mind (psychological) and brain (physical). Thus, understanding the structure of the physical brain and how trauma can impact it is essential to helping the client heal. As discussed in Chapter 1, those who have been exposed to ongoing trauma experience brain recon-figuration. In a nontraumatized brain, when the body senses a possible threat, it routes this information to the cortex for processing to determine if there truly is a threat. However, in a brain that is continually exposed to trauma, the brain learns to bypass the frontal cortex. Adolescents are especially vulnerable to these impacts because their frontal cortex is still evolving. Ms. Martin notes that when trauma occurs in childhood or ado-lescence, there may not have been adequate time for a pretrauma person-ality to develop. As noted in the first chapter, adolescence is a time of risk taking and exploration, due in part to the still-evolving cortex. When an adolescent is exposed to ongoing trauma, especially when it is linked to substance abuse, the limbic brain is in charge as it rules all three of these systems: the traumatized brain, the adolescent brain, and the substance abuse brain. Therefore, Ms. Martin's treatment model, discussed later in this chapter, is geared toward helping bring the prefrontal cortex "back on line."

The different parts of the limbic system are in charge of processing mental and emotional stimuli, including attachment to others (Applegate & Shapiro, 2005). Exposure to trauma appears to impact the hippocampus (the part of the limbic system in charge of memory), reducing it in size and affecting its ability to operate as it should. This affects a person's ability to recall events, causing them to be fragmented or completely for-gotten. The experience, however, may still be stored in the amygdale—in charge of danger and our response to it. This means that while a person may be unable to retrieve the memory, it can still impact the person through intrusive emotions, urges to flee, flashbacks, or bodily sensations (Applegate & Shapiro, 2005; D'Amico, 2014). Repeated exposure to stress also affects chemical reactions in the brain, rendering the person more sensitive to potential threats. Changes in brain chemistry are even more pronounced in children and youth because their brains are still de-veloping (D'Amico, 2014). Children who grew up in poverty or experi-enced maltreatment—two groups at high risk for trafficking—will already have started experiencing these impacts as a result of those experiences (see Chapter 1). Trafficking only worsens what has already begun.

In response to stress, many people are familiar with the "fight-or-flight" response. However, if the person is unable to do either, the body may attempt to protect itself by disassociation, often in addition to the hyper-arousal state of fight-or-flight. Disassociation prepares the body for injury by slowing the heart and breathing and releasing opioids to increase numbing and reduce pain (D'Amico, 2014). In situations where a person is repeatedly exposed to stressful situations, and these responses are continually triggered, these reactions may start to appear even without the stressful trigger and can have multiple negative impacts, including on memory (D'Amico, 2014). These impacts on memory are important to note because if survivors are asked to recount their experiences for the purposes of prosecution, if there are gaps or inconsistencies in their story, this may be seen as a sign of untruthfulness or unwillingness to assist, when it is likely due to the biological impacts of traumatic stress.

Arden and Linford's (2009) next letter in the BASE model is A for Attunement. Therapists, indeed all those who interact with a trafficking survivor, must make it clear to the client that they truly care, and they must be warm and empathetic. If they appear cold or uncaring, this will further feelings of shame and embarrassment in the client and can increase self-blame. Clients may have developed insecure attachment styles, and an appropriate therapeutic bond that reflects attunement with the client can help them develop a more secure attachment style.

The S in the BASE approach refers to the different Systems that must be considered. These include the family system, the social systems, diagnostic systems, and conceptual systems. Therefore, a full assessment of the client's context is necessary. The final letter, E, emphasizes that the therapist must use the best of what is known about what works in treatment— Evidence-based treatment. Just as we want our medical doctor making treatment decisions based on the best available research on what works, we want the same for our mental health. Practitioners must make adjustments based on the individual clients and their experience, but they should ground their approach in previously available empirical research as opposed to what they are most comfortable doing.

Psychological Impacts

Research has documented severe negative emotional impacts from being involved in prostitution. A study with a sample of adults, 21% of whom entered prostitution as children, found that 90% reported selling sex as a negative or traumatic emotional experience, reporting such emotions as feeling "sad," "dirty," or "numb" (Kramer, 2003). As noted, dissociation is a common coping mechanism among those who are prostituted in order to cope with these negative emotions. However, this can last long past the experience itself. Ross, Farley, and Schwartz (2003) found that even after being out of prostitution for 1.5 years, 22% of their sample still reported dissociation at an abnormal level. They state:

_____

Dissociation permits psychological survival ... Paradoxically, although the dissociative adaptation protects the person from the emotional impact of trauma, it increases the risk of further victimization since the survivor tends to dissociate in response to actual danger cues that are similar to the initial trauma. For example, even though she knows she is about to be betrayed, hit, or raped, she may not be able to mobilize other, healthier defensive strategies. (p. 205)

_____

Depression and low self-esteem are common psychological impacts, as are shame and guilt, as many blame themselves for their exploitation (Clawson & Goldblatt Grace, 2007; Hom & Woods, 2013). Many of these women come to associate their self-worth with their physical bodies (Hom & Woods, 2013). High levels of anxiety and fear are also common, and self-destructive behaviors, including attempts at suicide, may also present themselves (Clawson & Goldblatt Grace, 2007).

PTSD is common among those who have been involved in the commercial sex industry. Farley et al. (2003) found that about 70% of their sample met the criteria for this diagnosis. However, many clinicians working to help survivors recover believe this diagnosis is insufficient to express the experience of these survivors and will frequently refer to complex posttraumatic stress disorder (complex PTSD) or disorder of extreme stress—not otherwise specified (DESNOS) (Briere & Scott, 2013). In contrast to PTSD, which can result from a single incident, including a natural disaster, complex stress disorder results from "severe, prolonged, and repeated trauma, almost always of an interpersonal nature" (Briere & Scott, 2013, p. 41). Complex trauma can have a wide range of impacts, summarized in Box 4.1.

As noted in Box 4.1, complex trauma can result in many difficulties, physical difficulties as well as psychological ones, including attachment,

BOX 4.1 Domains of Impairment in Children Exposed to Complex Trauma

I. Attachment
  - Problems with boundaries
  - Distrust and suspiciousness
  - Social isolation
  - Interpersonal difficulties
  - Difficulty attuning to other people's emotional states
  - Difficulty with perspective taking

II. Biology
  - Sensorimotor developmental problems
  - Analgesia
  - Problems with coordination, balance, body tone
  - Somatization
  - Increased medical problems across a wide span (e.g., Pelvic pain, asthma, skin problems, autoimmune disorders, pseudoseizures)

III. Affect Regulation
  - Difficulty with emotional self-regulation
  - Difficulty labeling and expressing feelings
  - Problems knowing and describing internal states
  - Difficulty communicating wishes and needs

IV. Dissociation
  - Distinct alterations in states of consciousness
  - Amnesia
  - Depersonalization and derealization
  - Two or more distinct states of consciousness
  - Impaired memory for state-based events

V. Behavioral Control
  - Poor modulation of impulses
  - Self-destructive behavior
  - Aggression toward others
  - Pathological self-soothing behaviors
  - Sleep disturbances
  - Eating disorders
  - Substance abuse
  - Excessive compliance
  - Oppositional behavior
  - Difficulty understanding and complying with rules
  - Reenactment of trauma in behavior or play (e.g., sexual, aggressive)

(continued)

VI. Cognition
- Difficulties in attention regulation and executive functioning
- Lack of sustained curiosity
- Problems with processing novel information
- Problems focusing on and completing tasks
- Problems with object constancy
- Difficulty planning and anticipating
- Problems understanding responsibility
- Learning difficulties
- Problems with language development
- Problems with orientation in time and space

VII. Self-Concept
- Lack of a continuous, predictable sense of self
- Poor sense of separateness
- Disturbances of body image
- Low self-esteem
- Shame and guilt

Source: From Cook et al. (2005). Complex trauma in children and adolescents. Psychiatric Annals, 35(5), 390–398. With permission

behavior, and cognition. Examining these impacts, it is also clear why those who experienced maltreatment as a child are at higher risk for being trafficked as well as how being trafficked can result in these impacts.

Social Impacts

Social impacts, those that affect a person's social functioning but are not a psychological disorder, are also common. Amelia Rubenstein of TurnAround notes that having been trafficked can impact future romantic relationships. She works primarily with heterosexual females and thus notes that the sexual exploitation can affect intimate relationships in several ways. First, survivors often lack faith in their own judgment; they fear being tricked again. They may judge themselves and call themselves "stupid," for believing what they were told. Survivors also have concerns about future romantic relationships regarding when and how to share their abuse history with a new intimate partner and how the partner will react to or receive that information.

They may also be unwilling to trust others (Clawson & Goldblatt Grace, 2007). If they do not get the assistance they need to create healing, this can become truth, and they can fall into a cycle of manipulative relationships. Thus, Ross et al. (2003) note that helping survivors learn to trust their own judgment is an essential part of healing.

Females who have been prostituted may have a poor view of men, basing this on their experience with buyers and pimps. They may also have a difficult time being physically intimate as it may bring up traumatic memories for them, or they may struggle with hypersexualization as a result of their experience. Ms. Rubenstein notes that survivors may have to work to learn what actually pleases them sexually, rather than what they were told to do or act as if it pleased them. If dissociation was a coping mechanism for them, they need to learn how to stay present during intimate acts.

Services for Those Who Have Been Trafficked

In studies of commercial sexual exploitation of youth in New York City, the vast majority wished to leave the life—87% (Dank, 2011) and 92% (Dank et al., 2015). It should be noted that these studies included relatively few youth who were pimp controlled, and thus this number is likely an underestimation (Dank et al., 2015 specifically looked at those engaging in survival sex). However, youth noted numerous barriers to achieving this goal. To both recover from the trauma they have experienced and to be able to move forward in their lives, survivors typically need a whole host of services. This can include providing basic needs such as shelter and food, case management services, and mental and physical health treatment. Youth also need to develop skills that will allow them to support themselves, which may require education and job and/or life skills training. Services to help reunify them, physically and/or psychologically, with their families may be important in many cases.

However, accessing these services can be problematic. Although many lawmakers originally assumed that domestic survivors could easily access services available to all citizens, this is not the case. Many of these services require identification, and many survivors do not have their birth certificate or Social Security card to prove residency. They may not have had the opportunity to earn their driver's license, or it may have been taken from them.

Additionally, as important as these services are, it is at least as important to make sure they are delivered by the right people. When working with youth who have been trafficked, it is essential that providers understand the varied dynamics of trafficking and make youth feel that they can share the full extent of their experiences. While sex trafficking shares some components with sexual abuse, sexual assault, and domestic violence, it is distinct from these other traumas and so is its impact. It is necessary to understand complex trauma and the individual circumstances of that client's exploitation. A formerly exploited woman states that it is essential for providers to acknowledge clients as experts of their own experience (Hom & Woods, 2013). Tesy Molina of the Multicultural Counseling Center in Springfield, Virginia, states:

Their mind, their body, their spirit is completely broken. I think that's what makes it such a challenge. These are individuals who have been completely broken. Completely broken. And once you can understand that, then you can begin to understand how careful and how specific and how tailored the treatment needs to be for them.

One way to ensure that understanding is to have survivors as an integral part of developing and delivering services. There are survivor-run agencies, such as Courtney's House in Washington, DC, SAGE in San Francisco, My Life My Choice in Boston, and GEMS in New York City. Lisa Goldblatt Grace of My Life My Choice, who is not herself a survivor, but cofounded and coruns the agency with a survivor states:

We don't make any big decisions, we don't figure out what direction we're going, nothing happens absent that [survivor] voice being key in how we run the program. We really center the program around the idea of trying to elevate that voice; that should be the loudest voice in the movement, both adult women who were there as kids and kids who are there now.

If the agency is not survivor run, there are other ways to accomplish this, as discussed by Smith (2014). Providing a mentor who is a survivor provides the client with a personal connection to someone who was in the life and made it out. A connection with a survivor who is doing well can be a beacon of hope for one in the midst of the healing journey. To see that it is truly possible to make it out the other side can help a youth make it feel it is worthwhile to do the difficult work of healing. Lisa Goldblatt Grace states that "the mentors can bring the sense of hope that, if you haven't been there, you can't provide." SAGE notes survivors provide a positive role model in showing clients that people who were once in the same spot can live a "normal" life (Hotaling, Burris, Johnson, Bird, & Melbye., 2003). My Life My Choice also integrates survivor stories into their prevention curriculum as another method of inclusion, and the 10-session training is presented by a clinician in concert with a survivor. An essential piece of their program is that every survivor is paired with one of their staff who is a survivor for a one-on-one, long-term relationship. Lisa Goldblatt Grace notes:

The idea is that everybody needs a person as they recover; it's basic mentoring research. Our girls get bounced around a lot and every time they bounce, they lose whatever supports they had and so we felt for them to be strong there had to be somebody in their life that was consistent. So we travel to wherever they get bounced to, as long as it's within the state. And then we know that recovery takes a really long time, so it's voluntary, the services, but we'll stay in their lives as long as they want the support . . . Because it just takes a really long time.

Books written by survivors can also be used to help those on their healing journey. Smith (2014), in addition to her own book *Walking Prey*, recommends *Runaway Girl* by Carissa Phelps, *Girls Like Us* by Rachel Lloyd, and *The Slave Across the Street* by Theresa Flores. Staff who are not survivors can still serve as role models. Hotaling et al. (2003) state that seeing agency staff model positive relationships can also help in the healing process by helping them see what positive, healthy, respectful relationships look like. Providers can also provide a view of what "normal" life is like and why it is good. They can provide a view of the simple pleasures in the "square" lifestyle. Lisa Dingle of Youth For Tomorrow notes how to balance this with the therapeutic relationship:

Clients will sometimes ask about our lives outside of our work. They want to hear about normalcy. While there is a necessity for healthy boundaries in the therapeutic relationship, there are times when authenticity and honesty can provide increased trust and understanding. They will look at my family picture on my desk and imagine their own family picture someday, asking questions about what it is like to be a mom or a wife.

Case Management

Clinical intervention is not all that is needed to help survivors put their life on their own trajectory. As noted, the impacts of trafficking are diverse, and it is only by navigating a multitude of systems that survivors are able to access all the pieces they need. Many survivors need assistance in doing so, thus intensive case management is typically required. Tesy Molina states that the case manager must be the expert on these services; the clients will not necessarily be able to identify the issues for which they can receive services or where they need help accessing them. The case manager needs to ask the right questions and be able to refer not just to the right services, but to the right people within those services. For example, the wrong law enforcement officer may intimidate clients and make them afraid, causing them to close off, or may question the gaps in their memory. The wrong therapist may cause survivors to think all therapists will not understand their experience or will judge them for what they have suffered. A qualitative research study at GEMS has found that having a safe space for survivors, with people who do not judge them and help them to process the trafficking at their own pace (i.e., not time limited) is essential. Amelia Rubinstein of TurnAround in Baltimore notes that at her agency, as services evolved, they realized how different case management for this population was from other populations:

Case management here entails this transformational relationship. Because it's not just about case management. It's not just about the

referral. It's about, "this is my person and I can call her when I need
to." I have one girl who left a domestic violence situation, and he
asked her, "where you gonna go?" She said, "I'm gonna call my case
manager, 'cause my case manager will find me a place to go even if
I was in the middle of the woods." And so, just that kind of knowledge
that "I can leave an unsafe situation because I know someone will
help me find something else." So that's changed, like making sure
that case managers have cell phones. You can't just be tied to an
office phone.

The top three things youth felt they needed to leave the life can all
be linked together: steady employment, education, and stable housing.
Substance abuse treatment was also on the list, though much lower than
the others (Dank, 2011). This is echoed by the study by Farley et al.
(2003), which included adults, though the exact percentage is unknown.
They found that the top needs were housing (79%), job training (73%),
and substance abuse treatment (67%).

Melissa Snow, program specialist on child sex trafficking at the National
Center for Missing and Exploited Children (NCMEC), also assists with
support and recovery planning for children who are missing from care
and suspected of being exploited through sex trafficking. Because of the
high rates of system involvement (child welfare and/or juvenile justice)
common for those who are trafficked, they typically require services that
differ from other missing youth. She works with their caseworker or
whomever is the person coordinating their care, to educate them on trafficking and making sure specialized services are in place to reduce the risk
of re-exploitation. To accomplish this, she does "a lot of outreach, a lot of
awareness, a lot of coordination and a lot of advocacy to increase awareness of existing specialized services."

Amelia Rubenstein notes that she often needs to liaison with other
systems on behalf of the survivor. Law enforcement may have gathered
needed items from the survivor for prosecution, such as their phone or
ID. Survivors may need assistance from officers if the trafficker continues
to contact them even after they have left. Court advocacy is a related
area. If the case is prosecuted, it can sometimes take years from start to
finish. Survivors need help navigating the different steps of the criminal
justice process and assistance in getting benefits to which they are entitled, like restitution or crime victim compensation.

Returning to school can be another area with which case managers assist. Although case management with adults typically consists of just giving an address and directions, with these clients, it is usually necessary to go with them and assist them with paperwork and documentation. Because trafficking can be linked to poverty and economic need in many cases, it is essential to help survivors to develop the skills to support themselves. For clients who are considering attending college, help may be needed with applications and financial aid forms. Job training can also be needed. Job coaches can help with resumes or assistance in determining a career path. Life skills teaching can be offered, such as how to open a bank account or get an apartment.

Other services needed may not be as common as those who experience other forms of trauma. As noted earlier, many of those who are trafficked are tattooed as a brand of their pimp or gang. Continuing to wear that brand on their body can prevent them from being able to heal. Jennifer Kempton, herself a survivor of trafficking, has founded Survivors Ink to provide scholarships to help other survivors get their tattoos covered up. Tattoo artists donate their services to the project and only charge for their costs (Kelly, 2014).

Psychological Services

Helping survivors recover from the psychological impacts of being trafficked is difficult, complex work. Clearly, a therapeutic approach that was developed to help people resolve trauma is required when working with survivors of trafficking. Roe-Sepowitz, Hickle, and Cimino (2012) found that those with significant trauma symptoms had more difficulty in successfully completing treatment, underscoring the importance of a trauma-focused intervention. As detailed earlier in this chapter, the repeated trauma they have experienced, often layered upon trauma they experienced prior to trafficking such as abuse or bullying, has resulted in a host of negative impacts, and a careful approach is required to help them walk the journey of healing.

Clawson, Salomon, and Goldblatt Grace (2008) state that a trauma-informed approach is essential when working with trafficking survivors, and they note four components they see as essential to such an approach, understanding that: "Trauma is a life-defining event with a complex course which can profoundly shape a victim's sense of self and others;

The victim's complaints, behaviors, and symptoms are coping mechanisms; The primary goals of services are empowerment and recovery; and the service relationship is collaborative" (p. 5).

Thus, clinicians will typically use elements of trauma therapy, including trauma-focused cognitive-behavioral therapy (TF-CBT), integrative treatment of complex trauma (ITCT), or dialectical behavioral therapy (DBT). These therapies share several common components, which will be covered in general. For more detail, the reader is referred to the resources at the end of the book. Although the efficacy of these approaches with other populations has been validated in research, to date, research on the efficacy of treatment with those who have been trafficked is extremely limited.

TF-CBT integrates elements of other theories and approaches, including attachment theory and developmental neurobiology, into a cognitive-behavioral framework. The core values are summarized by the acronym CRAFTS (Cohen, Mannarino, & Deblinger, 2006, p. 32):

- Component based
- Respectful of cultural values
- Adaptable and flexible
- Family focused
- Therapeutic relationship is central
- Self-efficacy is emphasized

The components are summarized by the acronym PRACTICE (Cohen et al., 2006, p. 57):

- Psychoeducation and parenting skills
- Relaxation
- Affective modulation
- Cognitive coping and processing
- Trauma narrative
- In vivo mastery of trauma narratives
- Conjoin parent–child skills
- Enhancing future safety and development

However, TB-CBT may be ineffective for youth with externalizing behavioral issues, including substance use and "inappropriate" sexual behavior (Kliethermes, Nanney, Cohen, & Mannarino, 2013), creating caution for its use with survivors of trafficking.

ITCT builds on TB-CBT and also incorporates attachment theory and knowledge of trauma to focus on complex trauma; it can include a variety of modalities (exposure therapy, medication, etc.) as needed and monitors the effects of treatment throughout the therapeutic process (Lanktree & Briere, 2013). Dialectical behavior therapy also builds on cognitive-behavioral therapy concepts and includes a focus on mindfulness practices; it can be helpful in cases where behaviors counter-indicate the use of TF-CBT (DeRosa & Rathus, 2013).

Psychoeducation is a common element across the approaches. To understand what is happening, the client must be educated about the impact of trauma on a person. This helps to normalize the client's reactions. Many traumatized youth, trafficked or otherwise, have been the recipients of many negative labels (diagnoses such as oppositional defiant disorder or terms such as "difficult" or "demanding") and helping them to understand that their behaviors are a normal reaction to their experience can be a key step toward healing (Briere & Scott, 2013; Cohen et al., 2006). Lisa Goldblatt Grace notes that often "girls' trauma symptoms get interpreted as bad behaviors, as resistant, as delinquent" and understanding that can help lead to healing.

Teaching clients how to regulate the experience of their emotions is another common element. As discussed, repeated trauma causes changes in brain structure and chemistry that can swamp clients' ability to modulate their emotions. Psychoeducation can help the survivors to understand this and why regulation can be difficult for them. The therapist can teach them the skills of how to do so, which is needed for them to explore their experiences and to integrate their memories. Therefore, as named in ITCT, distress reduction (reducing acute, negative emotions) and affect regulation (developing the ability to regulate these emotions) are essential skills for clients to process their trauma and move toward healing. Relaxation and mindfulness techniques are key tools (Briere & Lanktree, 2012).

Integrating the concepts of adaptability and culture, it is important to emphasize that none of these approaches are formulistic. They all note that the approach must fit the client. Cohen et al. (2006) note that Latino children may experience *susto* (defined by them as fright or "soul loss"), where the soul may leave the body in response to a frightening event, while Native American children can develop *ghost sickness*. Briere and Lanktree (2012) also note the culture associated with socioeconomic status; many therapists are from the middle class, whereas those who have been trafficked may be from a lower socioeconomic class or have been living in that class while trafficked. Cultural norms such as how warmth and empathy are expressed or the importance of time can affect the therapeutic relationship.

If therapists are not survivors, they need to develop an understanding of the cultures that exist within the various forms of trafficking and to recognize that they *are* cultures. The nature of the trauma that survivors of pimp-controlled and gang-controlled sex trafficking experience is very similar; however, there are aspects of treatment that are different when someone has been gang involved. Megan Caesar of Youth For Tomorrow notes that helping a youth recover from gang trafficking can be even more complex than pimp-controlled trafficking. Some may be entrenched in the gang and have difficulty breaking the associations with the gang. Also, the family aspect of the gang creates a different dynamic than the connection with a pimp. It is not unusual for several generations of a family to be involved in the gang. The secrecy of the gang and unwillingness to trust outsiders also compounds the issue of working with gang-involved youth. Gang culture is not like other cultures.

This need for understanding of culture was echoed in the survey of programs conducted by Clawson and Goldblatt Grace (2007, p. 5) in which providers stated that "Staff must be culturally competent—knowledgeable about the culture of the street." If they are not survivors, they should not attempt to use the language of the street in order to try to develop rapport because as "squares," they will just look silly and actually impede rapport (Bender, 2013). Tina Frundt, executive director of Courtney's House in Washington, DC, and herself a survivor, explains:

It's like living on an island, right, so this is the United States.
But imagine you came to my island. My island has a culture. It has
laws. You may not agree with the laws or structure of my island at
all, but you just came onto my island. My island has a culture that
you don't understand and know. My island has rules, and unspoken
rules that you don't understand or know. You look on the outside and
judge my island and then you decide that it's done wrong. And so
now you rescue me from my island, and you took me away from my

island and you popped me into services. You said this is the right way
you're supposed to do it, but then get mad at me that I miss my home.
Because it wasn't a good island, you're absolutely correct. But it had
rules and procedures that were imbedded in my culture. So you can't
just plop me out and say you rescued me. I may have hated it. But
you don't even understand my rules. So for you to help me, you gotta
understand my rules, too. And show me what is wrong with the island.
Because I don't know. I was growing up on the island; I thought
everything was fine.

––––––––––

Part of culturally-appropriate services can be orienting services to the developmental level and gender of the client. Briere and Lanktree (2012) state that adolescence, though regarded as one developmental stage, actually encompasses several smaller developmental levels, and the approach must suit the level where the client is, which may not be the same as the client's physical age. They also note that gender roles can make certain emotions or experiences more or less acceptable to express; for example, female clients may be more likely to express fear, but less likely to discuss anger; male clients may be less likely to discuss experiences of sexual assault or victimization.

Tina Frundt of Courtney's House finds that not using traditional therapy terms helps her clients engage better with the services. Rather than a "therapy plan," her clients develop a "positive hustle." She works on explaining things to her clients in an easily understandable way. In the following excerpt, she shares her method for how she explains trauma and dissociation to clients:

––––––––––

So this is how we explain trauma in group. I ask them, "When you
were with the trick, at that moment, before you got into a car, before
you knocked on the door, did your head hurt? Did your stomach hurt?
Anything, any kind of sense?" Everyone either says, "My stomach hurt,
did a flip flop, my head hurt." "Ok," and I said, "Do you know what
that means?" They say no. And I say, "Well how often did it happen?"
"Every single time." "What did you do when that happened?" "Oh,
I pushed it deep down inside and I mainly think of something else."
I say, "Do you know what that's called?" "No." I say, "That's trauma."

So we can give signals with our body, our body is saying don't do it, don't do it. And we feel it and think ok, but I have to do it. Our brain is saying no, no, no, no, no, we have to do this. I say our stomach and our brain are arguing with each other, right, and they're like no, I have to do it. The brain is saying no, we're gonna push through. So I say it [that sense of trauma] didn't go anywhere, it has to hide in pieces of your body because your brain said no, this is what we're going to do. So I'm gonna pretend this isn't happening. So then the trauma says, ok well I'm gonna go hide right here in this little spot in the tummy, and that's where I'm gonna be. And then that's where it's hiding. So I'm like where did it go. They're like nowhere, it's just like laying there. Right. So let's talk about that. It's this big word I bet everybody heard here. I said who heard or spoke to a therapist and they say disassociation. And everyone raises their hands up. And they're like but I don't know what it means. Ok, so remember when the brain was having an argument with your tummy? They're like yeah. And that argument was like, ok we're gonna push past this one and do it anyway. But to do it I need to go to my happy pretty place. So everyone has their place they make up in their head to go. Ok, so that's that word the doctor was telling you. They're like, "Oh why didn't they just say that?"

Language is very important. At Courtney's House, they do use "real words," like "trick," but they do not use the word "rescue," as that puts the youth in a passive role and ascribes power to the "rescuer." Ms. Frundt states, "You can rescue a body, but not a mind." So at Courtney's House, the groups are called "Transitioning Your Mindset Out of the Life." She emphasizes short-term, rather than long-term goals with the youth. Many adolescents do not excel at long-term planning, never mind those who have been traumatized and focused on survival. They work on 1 day goals, then move to 2 days a week, until the client can get through the week, and then they move on to bigger goals. If the goals are too big and too long term, the client gets frustrated and then the goals can be a setup for failure. It is better to work on more immediate goals, give them a taste of success, before moving on to big goals. Top short-term goals of those at Courtney's House include being able to say no, being able to sleep (through the night, without lights, etc.), and having a good relationship with their parent(s).

Therapeutic Relationship

Clearly, when working with those who have been traumatized, and especially those who have been trafficked, safety and stability must be a concern. Clients will not be able to do the difficult therapeutic work if they do not feel safe and have some stability. Many things can act as triggers to remind the survivor of their experience. If they were trafficked from home, being in certain places in their neighborhood can act as triggers. Triggers may also include certain songs or being around men (Hom & Woods, 2013). Triggers include not only physical safety but also safety in the therapeutic relationship (Briere & Scott, 2013). All of the professionals who were interviewed emphasized how essential it is to always keep your word. This is true for any client, but especially for those who have had their trust violated so many times.

Reflecting the "A" for Attunement from Arden's BASE approach, the importance of the quality of the therapeutic relationship cannot be overemphasized. All of these therapeutic approaches note it as a key element, as did the providers interviewed for this book. Those who have been traumatized have had their ability to trust shaken; this is especially true for those who have been trafficked because their trust has been violated so many times. It has been violated in their past: if they were abused, bullied, rejected, and so on. If they had a trafficker, it was violated by them. If their trafficker was a family member, especially a parent, the impact is likely even more profound. Their trust was violated by the buyers. They likely have been told, and believed, that no one wants to help them and they cannot trust anyone. Thus, developing a relationship built on trust and respect is essential, but difficult. As noted by Briere and Lanktree (2012), the clients will likely test the providers, probably multiple times, to determine if they can truly trust them and if the providers will stay with them. Megan Caesar, a therapist with Youth For Tomorrow in Virginia, states the most important thing she has learned from her clients is that it is all about the relationship:

_____

The key is establishing a trusting relationship. Also, they want to know you're going to stick with them through the setbacks, because there will be setbacks at times. They want to know that if they do step backwards, the people who are working with them aren't just going to pull back, step away, and let them go.

_____

Genuineness of the therapist is also a key element of the trauma-focused approach. Clients know when a provider is not truly interested in them. Lisa Dingle states, "Survivors also want to laugh and joke with you and know that you care about them because you truly do care, and not just because it is your job to care." In addition, several providers interviewed emphasized the importance of having a relationship with the client where they feel they can share the worst of what happened and it will not shock the provider. This trust may be inherent if the provider is also a survivor; they know that person has been though similar things. If this type of relationship is not there, the client will hold back in sharing what occurred, and the necessary space for healing is not there. Hom and Woods (2013) note the experience of one survivor who was so shamed by her experience and worried about the reaction of the clinician that she had to get drunk in order to be able to attend the initial meeting. Briere and Scott (2013) note the importance of unconditional positive regard in working with trauma survivors and clearly communicating appreciation for the survivor's bravery (during the trauma and for coming to therapy) and the belief that the survivor is doing the best that they are able to with the circumstances. Tesy Molina of the Multicultural Counseling Center states:

If you don't understand, you won't even get anywhere with the victim if you don't understand where they're coming from. If you don't understand their trauma bond, if you don't understand their loyalty to their trafficker, their loyalty to the gang, right there they are going to put up a wall, and say, "I'm done. You're not gonna understand me, so why should I bother talking to you about this?" If a provider says, "So did you really love him? I mean, you didn't really love him. I mean, this man did so many things to you, didn't he? So how could you love him, you know? Are you sure you really love him?" Right there, that is who she depends on, that person worked so hard to get her loyalty that, right there, you're attacking the one person that she feels connected to.

One does not need to be a survivor to develop this trust and space for full honesty, but one does need to be clearly comfortable with whatever the clients may share of their experience. Amelia Rubenstein of

TurnAround notes, "We don't even feel comfortable talking to a regular 15-year-old about sex . . . you have to be able to hear really explicit things, and be okay, like let's pick this apart rather than, 'oh my gosh,' which is a reaction that they get really often." Ms. Rubenstein notes of the youth on her caseload, many had been in therapy right before or after they were trafficked. When she asked them if they discussed the trafficking with their therapist, they say, "No, I don't think she [the therapist] would get it." Ms. Rubenstein thinks that therapists would "get it" if they were trained and that it is essential to discuss "probably the most violent and horrific experience of this kid's life."

Not every clinician is able to do this work; clinicians must be able to truly connect with the clients and form a rapport with them. It requires not only advanced clinical skills but other qualities as well. Briere and Scott (2013) note that any therapist doing trauma work must be able to ask questions in a manner that communicates empathy and lack of judgment of the survivor. One formally exploited woman states that it takes "an enormous level of grace" to do this work and that the clinician must take the time to understand how the survivor feels and why she feels this way because this not only helps build trust but helps the clinician to truly understand the survivor's experience (Hom & Woods, 2013, p. 78). Ms. Molina notes essential characteristics include respect, being nonjudgmental, and the ability to be "real," as well as relaxed with the client. She states, "You need to know when to push and you need to know when to pull back." Clinicians should not push too hard or too fast with clients, but they do need to be able to get clients to the point where they are willing and able to do the hard work of opening up and starting the healing journey.

Few survivors will tell the whole story the first session. They are not sure they can trust the therapist, they are not sure they will be believed, and they do not know if the therapist can handle the details of what occurred. They may also not yet see themselves as having been exploited, or they may believe it is their fault, a result of their own poor choices. The impact of the trauma on their brain, as noted, has physically affected their ability to remember their exploitation. As noted, trauma experiences are not recorded as a simple story, with a clear beginning, middle, and end, but as a series of images. Thus, until they have progressed sufficiently in their healing to start processing their memories and work on reintegration, they may be unable to tell the full story. Bonnie Martin notes when working with fragmented traumatic memories, she may be working with the survivor's perception of what occurred rather than an "objective" memory. She states that this can make prosecution more complex as this perception may change as the survivor progresses in treatment. Thus, one role of the therapist is to explain trauma memory and fragmented narratives in court so a judge or jury can understand.

When working with any group that has been disempowered, it is important to give them power and control whenever possible so that they feel in charge of their own lives. Smith (2014) notes that an effective technique for her in her healing journey was when she was asked to write down her sexual encounters. She was not asked to discuss it out loud, nor was she asked to share the list, but it helped her think about some of the circumstances that led her into a trafficking situation. Ironically, the person who used this effective technique was not one of the mental health professionals, but an orderly in a psychiatric hospital. Hotaling et al. (2003) note that too often survivors are required to address their issues in the order required by the agency, rather than in the order important to them. For example, agencies may require that substance abuse be addressed prior to the receipt of other services, rather than recognizing that this use is driven by the other issues.

Sometimes this work can be done individually, and sometimes a group is a powerful way to create change; it depends on where the survivor is in the healing process. At GEMS in New York City, Julie Laurence, the chief program officer, states that girls may need individual therapy at first as they learn about sexual exploitation and begin to process what has happened to them. In New York, the Safe Harbor law (see Chapter 5 for explanation of Safe Harbor laws) only extends to age 16, so GEMS may have clients referred to them through the juvenile justice system who do not yet understand these issues. GEMS provides individual and group counseling, as well as connecting girls to survivor mentors and a supportive community to help them in this process.

Jessica Trudeau, the program director at GEMS, explains that GEMS runs three to five groups every day: educational, therapeutic, and recreational groups. They try to provide a range of options, such as yoga, music, art therapy, a book club, a current events group, and a self-esteem group. Their founder and CEO, Rachel Lloyd, who is a survivor, runs a survivors-only group once a week. All groups are voluntary, and the girls can choose the ones they enjoy and that fit with their schedule. GEMS has an incentive process where they receive $5 for each group attended. They maintain a timesheet that is signed by the group facilitator and turned in every 2 weeks. One week later, they will receive the monetary incentive. This helps teach delayed gratification as well as placing value on something besides their bodies.

GEMS then creates further opportunities for growth through their Youth Leadership program. A small set of girls are selected each year into the program, which is designed to create the next youth leaders in the movement to end commercial sexual exploitation. They go through a classroom-based curriculum that teaches them about sexual exploitation and all the factors that contribute to it. Afterward, they are eligible to apply for internships and fellowships at GEMS; some are eventually hired as staff members.

The usefulness of group therapy was supported in research conducted by Hickle and Roe-Sepowitz (2014). They describe the group developed for female adolescents they evaluated as having four essential components: educating participants about DMST; helping the youth help each other; addressing the shame and stigma participants experienced; and helping them learn to master their emotions, thus reflecting many of the elements discussed as core to trauma therapies—psychoeducation, attunement, and regulating emotions. They found educating the youth to be necessary because they were unaware of the crime of trafficking or that they had experienced it and used stories and scenarios to achieve this goal. The support offered by others who have experienced a similar situation is typically a primary reason for conducting a group intervention and that was true in this instance. Girls were often reluctant to share what had occurred to them, but the support and understanding of the other group members helped facilitate the healing process, which leads to the next point—addressing shame and stigma. Many of the girls blamed themselves for what they experienced and believed it was a consequence of their bad decisions. When they would share their stories in the group, other group members would counter this narrative and tell them it was not their fault, that blame belonged with the person who trafficked them. Because the group would bring up strong emotions, it was also necessary to teach the girls coping skills to manage these.

Residential Services

Residential services may be needed to help survivors concentrate on their healing work. This may be because they need a therapeutic environment or because their home environment may be dangerous or unavailable to them. Tesy Molina, who works with survivors of gang trafficking, many of whom are trafficked in their own neighborhood, states that her clients often need residential services at first:

They're not going to be able to recover if they're in the same neighborhood because everything's a trigger. For a client, she is driving down the same street, she is walking down the street, she has to probably glance at the corners where she was punched or kicked on the ground. She has to pass by apartment complexes where buyers went and solicited sex with her. So everything is retraumatizing. It's like there's triggers everywhere.

Clawson and Goldblatt Grace (2007) state that typically at least 18 months at a facility is needed to truly do the work and accomplish the goals, but full recovery can take much longer than this and should be available for as long as the survivor needs it. It takes an extended period of time for trust to be built, to process the experience and then build the supports and skills needed to move on from the trafficking. When interviewing providers, it was a common belief that youth should not be mandated to attend treatment, that it must be a voluntary choice. Unless the youth are invested in making the change, it will not work. Programs had a policy that if clients ran away from the facility, they were always allowed to return.

Because boys are not seen as being trafficked, few services have been developed for them, and even fewer residential placements will accept them. A 2013 survey found 28 beds across the country for male survivors (Reichert & Sylwestrzak, 2013). Gender roles may again play a role here because boys may be not only unwilling to identify themselves as having been trafficked but also unwilling to discuss the impact of the trauma they have experienced. Thus, even when they are identified, they may not present as having a need for services. This flat affect can also be a sign itself of trauma because PTSD can cause detachment (Figlewski & Brannon, 2013).

Many people have seen the need for dedicated residential services for sex trafficking survivors and have jumped in to help address it. The concern is that some of these groups do not have a background in social service provision, nor do they pause to consider options such as partnering with an existing agency that is already doing good work, conducting a needs assessment to assess if this service is needed in this area, or even speaking with survivors about what is needed. Tina Frundt, a survivor and executive director (and founder) of Courtney's House in Washington, DC, states that she frequently gets phone calls from groups seeking to establish residential facilities for survivors of domestic minor sex trafficking and finds that the question they most frequently ask her is whether or not the facility should have a pool. When she inquiries about treatment models or how they plan to meet state standards for children's residential care, they reply that they have not gotten to that. Although having space for recreation is important, it should not be the first item on a treatment center's list, but rather a potential part of the healing process.

When Bonnie Martin consults for those with residential facilities, she finds it essential to inform them about the impacts of trafficking and the concurrent trauma on the brain. Facilities may be located in a rural environment that is intended to be calming, but this can actually be very stressful to the adolescent who is accustomed to constant stimulation. They are used to constantly being in a state of hyperarousal and socialization, and if they are abruptly removed from that, it can be very stressful. Smith (2014, p. 149) notes that in her healing process, she wanted, "an active schedule with people talking to me." The brain has difficulty adjusting to the lack of energy and excitement. Clients start eating healthier at the center, which also affects brain chemicals. Therefore, it is essential that organizations have an understanding of these factors and develop services to meet them, to provide stimulation and excitement in a healthy fashion, such as sports.

Ms. Frundt states that ineffective services are harmful, not only because clients are not getting needed services, but a lot of money is being invested in these services. The potential clients do not want to go, because it is not designed to meet their true needs, and then the facilities close. This can lead some to believe that the services are not needed. In addition, when limited funding is allocated to ineffective programs, this means that it is not available for effective ones. Additionally, by focusing on residential facilities, it can exclude those youth who are living at home. Amelia Rubenstein notes, "It can be important for someone to go somewhere else and heal and come back, but these kids all return to their community, so how do you make that the healthiest place that you can?".

Thus, Ms. Frundt feels that a federal standard of care is needed. She states that this standard should be informed by the voices of survivors, especially those who have developed formal agencies. Housing requirements should be developed for residential facilities addressing sex trafficking much as they have been for domestic violence. She states that at domestic violence conferences, there is a track on housing that discusses programs, protocols, procedures, and licensing requirements, and that this is desperately needed for sex trafficking. However, she cautions, that when including survivors, it is essential to remember that every person's experience is unique. As noted in the previous chapters, there are different methods of trafficking, and even within the same general method, each person had their own unique experience.

Even at a residential facility that may be dedicated to servicing survivors of sex trafficking, they may not be trained in the different methods of trafficking or in the complex trauma that can result from the experience. Tesy Molina of Multicultural Counseling Services notes that she had a client who was at a residential facility for 2 years, but because the clinicians were not aware of complex trauma nor of how the dynamics of gang-controlled trafficking can differ from pimp-controlled trafficking, her client did not receive the appropriate services to recover from her exploitation and did not heal.

Services for the Family

A group who is often neglected in the development of services is the family of the child. Providers may assume that the child cannot return home, which may be a false assumption. However, even if it is correct, supporting survivors in reconnecting with their families and building a healthy relationship can be an important healing step and build support for the future (Clawson & Goldblatt Grace, 2007). Interventions with caregivers are core elements of the therapeutic interventions discussed earlier. Research from around the world of those who have experienced trauma has found that supportive relationships are an essential piece in the healing journey.

Bonnie Martin notes that current research supports the concept that "the environment post-trauma, the way the family responds to the traumatic incident can have more to do with how resilient that person is than the facts of the actual trauma itself." Illustrating the importance of a supportive family environment, lessons can be learned from working with another group of traumatized children: former child soldiers. Those who had support from their family and their peers were significantly more likely to have improved adjustment, including increased hope, decreased symptoms of PTSD, and better functioning (Betancourt, Borisova et al., 2013; Morley & Kohrt, 2013). On the other hand, former child soldiers who experienced stigma had their symptoms worsen (Betancourt, Newnham, McBain, & Brennan, 2013). Even in rats, when the mother rat and her children go through a traumatizing experience, if the mother feels able to help them afterward, the pups themselves have healthier functioning (Dobbs, 2012). Thus, it is essential to provide support to the family and others in the environment to which the youth is returning.

If the family does not understand what has occurred to the child, they may blame the child for the trafficking or go to the other extreme and place severe restrictions on the child's movements and actions in order to try to prevent a reoccurrence. The parents may also be trying to cope with their own guilt. If services are not provided to the family, these feelings can create an unwelcoming environment for the child, causing the child to leave and possibly return to the trafficking situation. Melissa Snow of NCMEC states that:

_____

When somebody goes missing or is exploited, there's impact within the entire family. And especially in situations of child sex trafficking, there's a lot of misconceptions that exist even within the family, that include blame, shame, and guilt, which can complicate the recovery process. Sometimes it can even create an inhospitable environment for a kid to return to and can actually increase the potential that they leave again just because they feel like they don't belong.

_____

Lisa Dingle of Youth For Tomorrow states, "The families are traumatized. They have been just as confused and just as hurt. However, it is possible that the families have not had treatment or access to resources that their child has had." Parents and other family members may also be triggered by things that remind them of the trafficking experience. Ms. Dingle explains:

Parents and loved ones are so scared and can be just as susceptible to triggers. For example, the youth might be on a home pass from our program, and an argument ensues. Their daughter might take on an attitude that reminds them of past rebellion that led down a path that ultimately resulted in pain and heartache for the entire family. Other triggers might include seeing their daughter in certain clothing or makeup, a request to spend time with an unknown male, engaging in the silent treatment to cut off communication, or not responding to a text or call when they are late for a curfew. For the parents, they feel the "uh-oh" deep inside that the trauma might happen all over again. This is why family therapy is such a vital component of treatment for victims, because the entire system has been traumatized and needs support.

Deepa Patel of Multicultural Counseling Services, clinical consultant on gangs and trafficking, also finds family therapy to be an essential component of her work. In her work, she has often seen parents believe that their child chose that life and that if they had not gone to that party or had not run away, none of it would have happened. Therefore, she works to educate the parent or guardian about the process of trafficking—the manipulation and the grooming. She sees this as an essential part of her work because of the negative impact on the children if their parents believe that they chose what happened to them. She works to help the family with any communication issues or troublesome interactions they may be experiencing.

At Courtney's House in Washington, DC, parent support groups are mandatory. These groups help the parents to understand what occurred and how to help their children, but also not to blame themselves. Because of the risk factors described in Chapter 1, people sometimes make the error of assuming that any child who was trafficked had a bad home life and bad parents. This puts the parents in a defensive place, while also trying to cope with their own self-blame. Youth want their parents to understand that it was not about them as parents; it was about an outside person.

The staff at Youth For Tomorrow also find it important to help the survivors feel comfortable discussing their experience with their parents. Although they do not need to discuss every detail, having the parents hear the story from their child's own mouth, rather than a professional, can be an important piece of healing the trauma for both the parents and the child. Another resource available at NCMEC through the Family Advocacy Division is Team Hope. This resource is available to family members who have a missing or exploited child, and it connects them with someone who has a shared experience who can provide support. Ms. Snow states:

Team Hope is a peer network for families, it consists of other families, both mothers and fathers and sisters and brothers who have experienced a missing or exploited situation within their family. And the idea is that obviously therapy is really important, but another component of service delivery is about connecting with somebody who has also been through the same thing, especially another mother or another father because they can have that kind of shared experience. So Team Hope is hundreds of these volunteers, parents or other family members who are currently going through some form of a missing or exploited situation but feel they have something to give back, or they have been through it and are giving a kind of hope and support to other families that are still going through this experience.

Examples of Services

Therapeutic Model

Bonnie Martin in her 15 years of working with survivors of trafficking has refined a model that focuses on a brain-based approach and draws heavily on the neuroscience of trauma and attachment theory. She has utilized the model in 13 different nations and found it to have cross-cultural applicability. Her model draws together information that has historically been in different mental health and medical "silos," in order to develop an approach that truly addresses the core needs of the trafficking survivor.

She named her approach SERVE: S—Symptom normalization; E—Education of the stress response; R—Regulation of body and thoughts; V—Validation of anger and grief; E—Empowerment of integrated self. Symptom normalization involves letting clients know that the symptoms they are experiencing are normal for the abnormal stress and trauma that they have experienced. She tells them, "All these symptoms, the cutting, the bedwetting, the impulse issues, the anger, the ADHD, the learning and memory issues, all of these things are normal, normal for abnormal stress."

Those who have been trafficked are often labeled as "bad" or "difficult" clients due to having a bad attitude, a bad temper, or seeming to not want help. They have gotten used to feeling that *they* are the problem. The therapist needs to assist the client with issues related to shame, anxiety, abandonment, and trust issues. It is essential that the therapist "avoid seeing survivors as 'poor little victims' or seeing their angry, acting-out behavior as the problem." Ms. Martin lets survivors know that what they are experiencing is normal, considering what they have been through. She says, "There is nothing wrong with you; there is something wrong with what *happened* to you." They have done what they needed to in order to survive and she helps them honor that:

I normalize those behaviors for them. Some say, "Oh they lie, they steal, they're manipulative." I reply, "Yeah, they do. How do you think they made it this far?" Everything they do that is maladaptive now helped them survive. We are dealing with a population who has survived horrific, horrific abuse. And they've survived. That's awesome. And so a lot of what I do is help my clients transition out of survival mode. I tell them that everything that helped you survive has now become maladaptive and is destroying you. So let's just focus on the fact that you're strong and you're resilient, and the lying, the manipulation, the stealing, doesn't go so well when you're in a residential home or on the job. So we discuss how they can replace those maladaptive coping mechanisms, but at the same time we honor the spirit of survival that has carried them this far.

Education consists of educating the client about how the brain works and how it reacts to trauma and stress. She informs them about the current

research regarding the brain, its reaction to ongoing stress, and how substances are frequently used to help moderate these stress reactions.

---

*We don't sit around and talk about "why do you cut, what's
the problem, why don't you love yourself"; that's not what we do.
We ask, "When you cut yourself the last time, did you feel like you
were really angry, hyperaroused, anxious, upset? Was your skin
flushed, was your heart beating really fast, what was going on? Or
were you feeling numb? Were you feeling cold? Were you feeling
bored? Or dissociated?" So this is the language we use. So you cut
because you were in that state and what do we do better the next
time? How can we find other means to deal with that stress in the
body without cutting?*

This education is an essential step to the next: Regulation of body and
thoughts. Once clients are aware of how they react to stress and triggers,
they can start to work on regulating these reactions. Regulation of the
body comes first and then regulation of thoughts. First, it is important to
help clients work on being able to calm their bodies. She teaches them
grounding techniques, such as progressive muscle regulation and deep
breathing, to help them regulate stressors without substances. Once they
can manage stress better in the body, she helps them learn to regulate
their thoughts, which is a more difficult process.

For many children who have "good enough" parents, they learn how
to calm themselves through their parents. Infants are not born with the
ability to self-soothe; they are calmed by their parents—parents who do
not smother them but also do not inflict pain on them or walk away or
neglect them either. However, as noted, far too many children do not
have this "good enough" parent, and they have never learned this ability,
nor learned how relationships can help heal. Attachment theory states
that children who do not learn to form secure attachments in their childhood with their primary caregiver(s) will be at higher risk throughout
their lives of struggling with forming healthy relationships. The relationship with the therapist can thus become a model for learning about

healthy relationships if the survivor has not previously experienced this. Ms. Martin notes:

The relationship with the therapist becomes the catalyst for the healing. It's in relationship that we're hurt, it's in relationship that we heal, and it may not even be having all the answers, but we can be present and mirror a new way of managing stress.

It is important that the therapist, as well as the others in the client's life, understand that the client has been operating in survival mode for at least the length of time they have been trafficked, if not before. This cannot simply be switched off. The client may have developed betrayal bonds with the traffickers and developed a sense of community and family. For those who are not trained in betrayal trauma, it can be very confusing and difficult to understand. An understanding of the development of these bonds—the hows and whys—is essential to combating them.

People cannot help that they are triggered—either biologically or psychologically—but they can regulate their reaction. Although many clinicians favor cognitive-behavioral therapy, Ms. Martin finds acceptance and commitment therapy for trauma to be a better fit for work with this population. She states that training in motivational interviewing is "absolutely critical for anybody who works with this population," together with a comprehensive understanding of the stages of change.

The V of the SERVE model is for Validation of anger and grief, which is often a new experience for her clients, whether they are teens who have just left the life or adults who left it many years ago. Many of her clients do not identify as having been victimized. Smith (2014, p. 155) states of her healing process, "Because I was unable to see that I was victimized, I was unable to see myself as a victim. I saw myself as an adult making decisions to survive."

Ms. Martin states it is essential to remember that healing is a spiral, and not a linear, process. It is important for both clients and therapists to remember that simply because a person is in a good place now, it does not mean the person will not be triggered by something 6 months from now. For many survivors, when they have their own children, they must work through the grief and anger again. She states some models empha-size forgiveness, and while that can be healing, she notes it is important to acknowledge that forgiveness does not mean the absence of anger and grief; these emotions are an important part of the healing process. Sometimes she is the first person to express anger or sadness about what happened to them, and this gives them room to be angry or sad about it as well.

The final letter of the SERVE model stands for Empowerment and works to help survivors integrate their experience into their psyche. Survivors can be caught either in a place where they push away their ex-perience and insist they are fine, despite the impacts impeding their life, or it overtakes them and defines their identity. Ms. Martin helps them to acknowledge the trauma, but not to allow it to define them. This empow-erment also helps enables them to avoid future exploitive relationships.

Community-Based Model

In Dallas County, Texas, girls entering through the juvenile justice system who are identified as exploited or at high risk for exploitation are referred to the Letot Center and its special court E.S.T.E.E.M. (Experiencing Success Through Encouragement, Empowerment, and Mentoring). Connie Espino, field probation officer with the program, explains that this is a wraparound diversion program developed as a result of action by the Juvenile Detention Alternative Initiative subcommittee, as the ju-venile judge wanted to assist this population that she kept seeing in her court. The girl must be on or beginning deferred prosecution or postad-judication probation services and have at least 4 months left because the program lasts about 4–6 months.

The judge utilizes the court process as an important part of the pro-gram. The first time the girl comes to court, the judge introduces the staff (herself, the baliff, the probation officer, and other staff). These profes-sionals are the same ones every Wednesday (court day), and it helps de-velop support for the girl and not merely be a punitive process. Similar to that previously noted with Maryland State Police, the Dallas County police work to be a positive presence in the girl's life. Ms. Espino notes that the officers will come to the Center to talk to with the girls and bond with them. She notes that the officers keep their word to the girls and are responsive to the parents. The strength of the bond can be seen when the girls say such things as "That's my detective."

This step-level program has four levels, each intended to last 30 days in duration, but can last longer if needed. It incorporates many of the aspects previously including a weekly support group—the HOPE group (Helping Overcome and Prevent Exploitation), a mandatory parent support group, and home-based family therapy. They also have enrichment activities, based on what the girls say they want to do, such as visits to museums, the aquarium, and the opera, as well as a mother–daughter etiquette class. The group helps them see the similarities between their situation and that of the other girls, and they realize they are not the only ones who have experienced this type of situation and this reduces the isolation and self-blame.

Because they are in the juvenile justice system, girls in the program have several checks and supports. Their attendance at school is checked and a GPS tracker monitors their routes. They must come to court regularly to check in; how often depends on what level they are on. Wednesdays are the day for this program, and a girl on Level 1 must come all four Wednesdays. Level 2 girls come three Wednesdays, Level 3 girls come two Wednesdays, and Level 4 girls come once a month. The program used to provide a mentor, but their previous partnership has not continued and they are seeking a new one.

The support of the family, especially the parent(s), is essential to healing. Ms. Espino has found that if the parent is not invested, the girl may try, but then "fizzle out." The message that an uninvolved parent sends to their daughter is that it isn't worth it. The process isn't worth it; the girl isn't worth it. The girl then figures, if they aren't invested, if they don't care, why should I? Therefore, the parent group is mandatory in order to assure the girls' success. Ms. Espino has found parents may be resistant at first, but then they often become invested. The program works to help develop family bonds and supports by taking families on retreats and doing a ropes course with parents. All girls currently live at home, but the center will soon open the Letot Girls' Residential Treatment Center, though this will still be limited to those involved in the juvenile justice system. The downside to this model is that girls must be adjudicated in the criminal justice system in order to receive services, which as noted, can increase their sense of self-blame. However, it does help ensure safety and the provision of services.

Residential Model

At the Youth For Tomorrow residential center outside of Washington, DC, they also find a mix of individual, group, and family therapy to be an effective combination for healing. According to Lisa Dingle and Megan Caesar, therapists at the center, the group—Girls on a Journey—helps survivors heal because it involves girls at different stages of the healing process, and therefore they can learn from one another on issues such as coercion, rebuilding their self-esteem, and just sharing what has helped them. They have also observed that as girls heal, they come to a point when they no longer want to discuss their experience, but instead they want to focus on the future and gain skills to help them succeed. However, as girls progress in their treatment, they are willing to retell their story for the specific purpose of helping girls who are earlier in their treatment; the girls move into a leadership role. Ms. Caesar notes:

———————

They're able to identify with one another's experiences. Recently we have had a few girls who have gone through a lot of individual therapy and have really grown in their healing process and they've been able to even lead some of the groups, come up with discussion topics they would like to discuss with the girls, share things in group, that have created a really interesting dynamic where they become the leaders and they're able to speak to the lives of the girls from personal experience.

———————

Ms. Dingle recalls examples:

———————

Recently, a young lady was about to be discharged. It had taken her a while to feel comfortable sharing her story with peers, but she felt like now that she was about to leave, she wanted to leave some words of wisdom to the younger girls. We also have another young lady who had a song she wanted to share at the next group, because the song had really helped her. They are eager to share resources, "this has helped me, maybe it will help you."

———————

Self-Care

An important closing note is the prime importance of self-care, an issue raised during interviews by many of the professionals working in the field.

This work is difficult and distressing, and there is a high risk for burnout or collapse if professionals do not care for themselves as well as they care for clients. If this is not done, there can be a high turnover rate, which is very harmful for clients, who already have experienced extensive abandonment and broken trust in the past. Ross, Farley, and Schwartz (2003) underscore this, stating that the therapy cannot proceed unless the therapist has an ongoing means of addressing his or her reactions to the survivor's trauma.

Bonnie Martin noted that good boundaries are essential, carving out time when you do not answer your work phone or answer your work e-mail. Many therapists themselves have experienced trauma, but they need to have done their healing work and be in a good place currently in order to provide clients with the necessary services. She also stated that laughter and a healthy family life are essential to creating balance. She says, "You can't have drama in your personal life and drama in your professional life. You get to choose, but you shouldn't have both."

For example, Connie Espino noted that positive activities are a must for her, such as hiking and taking time off, as well as a good social support system in family and friends to provide more positive experiences to balance out the stress from this work. Many providers talked about the importance of a colleague who "gets it," someone they can discuss the issues with which they are dealing who knows the dynamics of working on this issue and with this population. Having good supervision and knowing that one can reach out for support whenever needed was also noted as a key piece. Ross et al. (2003) state that good supervision is essential to prevent secondary traumatization as well as to make sure their responses to the survivor's experience do not impede the healing process. A provider interviewed by Macias-Konstantopoulos et al. (2015, p. 12) stated:

People think they can just handle trauma work. We deal with trauma all the time in our work, but if you really want to get into somebody's trauma, this is very delicate, specialized sort of, kid gloves kind of slow process, and really [you need] people that are skilled in knowing the nuance of that kind of treatment.

At GEMS, they make sure this is done on both the individual as well as organizational level. Because they recognize that therapy is important for staff to cope, but it can be hard to make time with both job and personal life responsibilities, they allot all staff an hour a week to do this. They also ensure supportive supervision, as well as good health care and vacation policies.

Survivors also note that self-care is important for them as well. The SEEN Youth Advisory Board (comprised of youth participants from the My Life My Choice Leadership Corp) offer suggestions such as relaxing by going to a movie or listening to music. They can get their nails done, watch sports, exercise, create poetry or art, or engage in a hobby. They can also reach out to other girls and share support with each other or speak with a mentor.

Conclusion

This chapter has discussed what practitioners have found to be important elements in helping survivors heal from trafficking. Many common elements were found across the various service models and providers that discussed the impact of trauma and how to address it effectively. A trusting relationship with the survivor was a core concept, as well as an understanding of trauma and therapeutic techniques to address it. Key to this healing is providers' ability to take care of themselves. A lot of good work is being done, but much more remains; this is the topic of Chapter 5.

5

What Needs To Be Done

Although attention to domestic minor sex trafficking is increasing exponentially, much work remains. It is important to focus efforts on key areas to be most effective, both in prevention and recovery. We need to develop effective laws to address this crime and punish its facilitators. We need to develop programs and services to assist those who are being trafficked in being identified and in receiving services to help them heal, and to train professionals to provide these services effectively. We must also look at prevention: What can be done to prevent children from being sold for the sexual pleasure of others? What can be done to stop people from buying them?

Focus on Perpetrators

Without those who facilitate the crime—buyers and those who control trafficked youth—it would not exist. It is a basic capitalist principle; if there is no one to produce the "product," and if there is no one to buy it, it will not exist. Thus, in order to understand why this crime exists, and therefore how to stop it, it is necessary to understand the facilitators.

The Exploiters

Little research has been done with exploiters themselves, and what work has been done has focused on pimps as exploiters, not gangs or family members. This section draws on the work of two reports, Raphael and Myers-Powell (2010) and Dank et al. (2014), both of which interviewed former pimps. Raphael and Myers-Powell used a snowball sample of 25 former pimps in Chicago, while Dank et al. interviewed 73 incarcerated pimps in eight cities around the country. In both studies, the pimps were primarily Black men. The stereotype that pimps are Black men and Black men are pimps can even be found among Black pimps themselves. Smith (2014) notes that one of the rules enforced by her pimp was that she was not allowed to speak to any Black men because "most of 'em are pimps" (p. 10).

The participants in these studies identified pimping as a way to make money, and the concept of selling sex was normalized by the activity of family members and neighbors. In both studies, selling sex, both themselves and by others they knew, was common; 100% of the women had sold sex themselves before becoming a pimp, while in Raphael and Myers-Powell, 56% of the men had done so. Dank et al. did not discuss whether the men in the study had sold sex, but they did note that a third of them had family members who were involved in pimping or selling sex. Sixty percent of those in the Raphael and Myers-Powell study reported family members involved in prostitution. Both samples also reported high levels of involvement by neighbors in commercial sex with the internalized message being that "one should be paid for sex and that sex would provide monetary benefits" (Raphael & Myers-Powell, 2010, p. 2). These pimps often came from low-income neighborhoods; thus, this was a way to make money in an area that had few other means of doing so (Dank et al., 2014). In the study by Raphael and Myers-Powell, many did not have high levels of education, and two thirds of the sample had not completed high school; however, in Dank et al., this was only 20% of the group.

Both studies found that there were many common elements between those who are prostituted and those who prostitute them. Raphael and Myers-Powell found that an overwhelming percentage of their sample reported physical abuse as a child (88%) and childhood sexual assault (76%) and that half reported running away from home due to this abuse. There were also high levels of family dysfunction, with 88% reporting intimate partner violence in their childhood home and 85% noting substance abuse. Eighty-five percent noted regular alcohol use themselves, with the average starting age being 12 years. A quarter had been in foster care.

Pimps saw themselves as "business managers," and they regarded their duties as overseeing those in their "stable"—training and instructing them, managing the money, and ensuring safety (Dank et al., 2014). They also had other employees to assist them, including drivers and the bottom girl (Dank et al., 2014). As discussed in Chapter 2, bottom girls are those who are given some level of responsibility over the other girls the pimp manages. She has sold sex herself and understands how the pimp operates. In some cases, she may be the mother of his children. She may help him recruit and train new girls (Dank et al., 2014). For example, one woman who was first turned out at age 12 by her mother, herself a prostituted woman, and later controlled by a pimp, was offered the opportunity to stop selling herself by the pimp if she would recruit other girls. She stated:

I have been pimped all my life, used by my family, and sold to any Johnny-come-lately. I was tired of selling my own body. It wasn't my idea at first, but I knew all the ropes and the girls trusted me. (Raphael & Myers-Powell, 2010, p. 3)

Some of these bottom girls may be regarded as pimps themselves. They may be coerced by threats of violence into taking over the work if the pimp goes to jail, and they may have to collect the money from the other girls so the man is never arrested as a pimp, since they never gave any money to him.

Pimps may also employ drivers to transport the girls between "dates." They may have a secretary to help with scheduling, depending on the complexity of the operation. Some even hire a security team (Dank et al., 2014). They may pay off law enforcement, hotel staff, or convention center staff in order to avoid detection or gain referrals. Because of this web of those who are complicit, together with the high number of buyers, pimps saw their business as acceptable and safe (Raphael & Myers-Powell, 2010).

Even when they are arrested, there are barriers to prosecuting the traffickers, as assessed by Reid (2013). As discussed earlier, many of those who have been trafficked have psychological ties to their trafficker and do not view themselves as a crime victim. Regardless of whether it is a pimp, a gang, or a family member, these bonds of loyalty and commitment can make the survivors unwilling to assist in a criminal prosecution of their traffickers. Even if survivors are willing, fear of the traffickers may inhibit them from participation as well. Additionally, if survivors have been arrested previously and charged with a crime, while the facilitators and/or johns were not, this enforces the idea that law enforcement is not to be trusted. Sometimes, even if law enforcement is not seeking to charge them, if the officers take them off the street, there may not be a facility in which to place survivors other than a juvenile justice facility, further reinforcing the perception of themselves as criminals.

There can be barriers within the legal system as well. Even when there is evidence of trafficking, perpetrators are often not charged with trafficking offenses, but rather charges related to promotion of prostitution. Prosecutors can be wary of charging someone with those offenses due to the lack of precedent and case law on trafficking charges; they prefer to use charges with which the judge and/or jury are more familiar in order to secure the conviction. This can lead to reluctance on the part of law enforcement to investigate cases of trafficking because they are not prosecuted (Farrell et al., 2012).

Despite prosecution difficulties, the attention being paid to domestic minor sex trafficking has been having an effect. As more focus has been placed on this crime, facilitators are getting the message. More and more pimps are turning away from using children. Several law enforcement officers interviewed noted that some pimps are even now asking for ID to prove that the female is over 18 because they have learned that prosecutors consider these cases a "slam dunk" because they do not have to prove force, fraud, or coercion. Special Agent Morlier of the Department of Homeland Security notes that prosecutors prefer cases with minors, "because they don't have to teach the jury what coercion is, if they can show someone's age, if they can show them a birth certificate [it's easier]. They prefer to go with something they can easily prove." Corporal Heid in Maryland stated that one pimp told him, "I can get in a lot of trouble if we had a juvenile, so I make everybody show me their ID."

Dank et al. (2014) found that in Miami, for example, law enforcement officers stated that they were seeing the numbers of minors on the street going down. This is not an unqualified success, however, because the pimps were simply replacing them with those over 18; they may also be selling them online. Trafficking is a crime against those of any age, but it can be harder to prove for those over 18. One former pimp stated,

"Honestly, you just have to stay away from minors. I've never known a pimp that got in trouble for messing with adults. Law enforcement focuses on minors" (Dank et al., 2014, p. 146).

It is important to note the pimp's comment that no one gets in trouble for prostituting those over 18. Although the work being done to address the sex trafficking of minors is absolutely essential, it is also critical to remember that these factors affect those over 18 as well. Many adults working in the sex trade started as children. Corporal Chris Heid of the Maryland State Police says, "We've identified a ton of girls 18, 19 years old, they've been doing it since they were 15, 16 years old. These girls are not just starting that day that we pick them up at 18 years old. They're starting a couple years before that."

Also, because pimps are realizing that it is becoming increasingly easy for them to be prosecuted for trafficking of those under 18, they look for 18 and 19 year olds. These youth typically have the same vulnerabilities and experience the same deleterious impacts as those under 18, but they do not have the same protections under the law. This is especially true for youth aging out of foster care. States are working to extend supports past the age of 18, but for many, they are on their own after 18. Donna Gavin, lieutenant in Boston Police Department and the commander of the Human Trafficking Unit, states the majority of cases with which she works are youth who have aged out of the child welfare system:

They've grown up in foster care, they've lived in group homes, they've run away from those homes since they were 14, 15. They have no high school education. Basically, there's no safety net. When it's a juvenile, there's usually a safety net, the Department of Children and Families has services. But when these kids turn 18, there's nothing for them, so oftentimes there's a crisis. There's not a whole lot for them.

The Buyers

In addition to those who traffic youth, attention must be given to those who buy them. Shared Hope International (2007) conducted a study looking at marketplaces of victimization from a demand perspective, and it compared Japan, Jamaica, the Netherlands, and the United States. Melissa Snow, formerly employed at Shared Hope, operated as a primary researcher on this project and notes that what the research found is that the marketplaces are absolutely demand driven. In reflecting on that research she states, "Anywhere that you're going, the marketplace of illegal, legal, and tolerated commercial sex is set up just like any type of shopping situation where it's going to the access point and the availability, the price point, all of these things are based on what the buyer is communicating they want and expect." She states that looking at the buyers can be an "uncomfortable conversation" for people because we are talking about thousands and thousands of people in our own communities, who most would view as everyday citizens: men with families, who work 9-5 jobs, and coach sports or attend your local church. Ms. Snow says, "It's easier to stigmatize pimps or to talk about the issue of sex trafficking overseas and ignore the issue happening in your own community. But when we talk about who the buyers are, if it's within our own community, that becomes more of a challenge."

Research has found that there are different types of buyers who purchase sex with a minor. There are opportunistic buyers who do not care what age the person is—35 or 15—while others purposefully seek out children. Some law enforcement officers believe that buyers seek out children because they believe they are less likely to have sexually transmitted diseases (Dank et al., 2014).

Pimps state that buyers are all ages, genders, socioeconomic statuses, occupations, and races. They even report instances in which wives would call them to arrange a meeting for their husbands (Dank et al., 2014). This research into the characteristics of buyers is supported by Shared Hope International's study in which, of the 407 cases they identified, the age of buyers ranged from 18 to 89 and 99% were men (four were women). For the subset of 137 cases where the buyer's profession was identified, almost 20% worked with children in some capacity such as a teacher, coach, Boy Scout leader, or military recruiter, while 22% were in a position of authority or trust such as law enforcement, military, or ministry. In 2014, law enforcement officers across the country coordinated the "National Day of Johns Arrests," and almost 500 people were arrested, as well as 14 traffickers. One mother was arrested for attempting to sell her 15-year-old daughter, and a border control agent in full uniform was arrested for attempting to purchase sex (Alter, 2014).

Victor Malarek, author of *The Johns: Sex for Sale and the Men Who Buy It* (2011), interviewed buyers and found that many have convinced themselves that women have actively chosen prostitution, make a lot of money doing it, and enjoy it. The buyers in his study stated that unless they saw a physical chain on someone, they believe she is freely choosing to sell herself. Pimps also feel that buyers like to maintain the illusion that the girls are working on their own to meet the bills and support this by having the girls put them (the pimp) in their phone contacts under the name of another female in order to maintain the illusion that they are not under the control of someone else (Dank et al., 2014). However, in the study by Farley et al. (2011), men who bought sex were just as likely to be aware of the coercion experienced by most women in the sex trade as men who did not buy it, but this did not deter the buyers. Farley et al. (2011) found that men who bought sex were more likely to have criminal histories, have higher self-reported likelihood to rape women, and acknowledged fewer harmful effects of prostitution.

Buyers have typically not faced the full legal charges that could be brought against them. Shared Hope International (2014) states that this can be due to the perception that arresting a buyer does not truly affect trafficking, while getting a pimp off the streets does. However, as they note, this perception relied on the assumption that each buyer is a one-time customer and that no one will step in to fill the void left by the arrest of a pimp. However, both of these assumptions are false.

It was not until 2010 that the first buyer was indicted for sex trafficking of a minor. This case was in Missouri and was the result of a sting operation known as Operation Guardian Angel. Law enforcement posted an ad online that stated, "While there mommas away these girls will play. My girlfriend is out of town her daughters are ready to play with you. Be the first for the little girls ..." (Department of Justice, 2009, para. 5, sic). The statement that the supposed children were in fact children was explicitly stated so that the buyer could not claim he did not know. The buyer received 10 years in prison without the possibility of parole ("OP man sentenced," 2010). However, prosecution of buyers has been rare.

Shared Hope International (2014) conducted a study assessing the outcomes for buyers over a 5-year period (2008–2013). Some of these come to the attention of police through a sting operation, such as placing a fake ad on the Internet as in Missouri. Others are arrested in the act of attempting to purchase an actual child. They found that in 134 cases that they assessed, 119 buyers were arrested, 118 were prosecuted, and 113 were found guilty. However, of the 112 who were originally charged with commercial sexual exploitation of a child, only 44 had that included in their final charge, a reduction by 60%. While 15 faced only a charge of solicitation of prostitution originally, this more than doubled to 38 in final charges. The other charge that supplanted the CSEC charge was sexual abuse of a child. No buyers were charged with trafficking.

However, the 2015 Justice for Victims of Trafficking Act will help address this. This Act specifically states that buyers are considered as culpable as traffickers for sex trafficking offenses. This concept was included in the original TVPA by use of the word "obtains," and as noted, some buyers have been prosecuted accordingly. However, confusion continued and thus this new Act added the words "solicits or patronizes" to emphasize that those who purchase others are also guilty of trafficking (Shared Hope International, 2015).

Traditional penalties for buyers have included shaming techniques, seizing of the car or driver's license suspension, or community service requirements (Shively, Kliorys, Wheeler, & Hunt, 2012). The men interviewed by Farley et al. (2011), both buyers and nonbuyers of sex, stated that public shaming would be an effective deterrent—including being placed on a sex offender registry or being named in a public place such as a billboard, the Internet, or newspaper.

However, those interviewed for the Shared Hope report note that "we cannot prosecute our way out of this problem" (2014, p. 38). They state that in order to truly deter buyers and thus reduce domestic minor sex trafficking, the perception that prostitution is a victimless crime needs to change. They believe that the current "cultural tolerance" around the purchase of a person for sex facilitates trafficking by excusing the behavior of buyers, resulting in lower penalties for them. The general public, as well as buyers, needs to be aware of the devastating impact that this crime can have, and that buyers are central to causing this harm. This knowledge may deter some buyers from engaging in this crime. Additionally, if greater stigma can be created around purchasing children for sex acts, this can also act as a deterrent to potential buyers.

Educational interventions are one way to do this—these can be primary prevention focused (community awareness) or tertiary (focused on those who have been arrested, known commonly as "john schools"). "John schools" are typically 1-day programs designed to address the misconceptions of buyers, for example that prostitution is a victimless crime, that most women are freely choosing to do it, and that they make a lot of money. They also discuss health and legal consequences. Mandating attendance at this program may be in lieu of, or in addition to, sentencing from the court (Shively et al., 2012). Kennedy, Klein, Gorzalka, and Yuille (2004), at the end of the john school that they assessed, found significant changes in attitudes toward prostitution, women who were prostituted and toward purchasing sexual services.

Cities Empowered Against Sexual Exploitation (CEASE) works in cities around the country to help reduce demand. In some cases, this involves arresting buyers, as opposed to those who are prostituted. There is also an educational component; for example, in Phoenix, they created fake ads for commercial sex. When the would-be buyer phoned, they spoke with a police officer who informed them of the damage that commercial sex causes to those who are sold and that the police will be focusing on buyers. Ninety-eight percent of the callers stayed on the line to listen to the whole message, and 68% gave a positive response about how it affected them (Demand Abolition, n.d.a). In Seattle, there are online ads about the harms of prostitution and penalties for purchasing sex that pop up when search terms are used in a search engine relating to purchasing sex, especially with a minor (Demand Abolition, n.d.b).

Focusing on primary prevention, since the vast majority of buyers are men, teaching boys that people's bodies are not commodities will help drive down the demand side. If we help young people understand what a healthy relationship looks like, and to challenge traditional stereotypes of masculinity, as noted by Melissa Snow, that will help. She notes how the purchase of child pornography has been heavily stigmatized within our society and substantial penalties result from the possession of child pornography and that we need to do the same for those who exploit the child in person. As one example, the Chicago Alliance Against Sexual Exploitation (CAASE) has created a program for high school boys to change the idea that buying people is normal and acceptable. They educate these youth about the realities of the sex trade and the role men play in perpetuating it, with the goal of preventing them from ever engaging in it (Burque, 2009).

Linking back to the societal factors discussed in Chapter 1, Malarek (2011) states that society is complicit in men purchasing others for sex. Society has accepted the belief that men must have sex and that prostitution is an "acceptable outlet" (p. 15) and seen as harmless. These men may be fathers purchasing someone for their sons, men at bachelor parties, men at business meetings, or other groups of men in which purchasing people for sexual pleasure is seen as acceptable. According to studies he cites and buyers he interviews, men are paying to have sex without the burden of the expectations that come with having sex in a relationship: to a woman devoted solely to their desires, rather than reciprocity, and to be able to walk away afterward. Malarek states these men view women as a "disposable commodity" (p. 54)—to be used and thrown away. They feel entitled to do whatever they want to them, even if it hurts them.

Thus, if trafficking is to be stopped, sexism and exploitation of women must also be addressed. Images of women and girls in the media need to be addressed (see the work of Jean Kilbourne). Girls need to feel they have avenues to earn money other than through their bodies, meaning that the gender pay gap needs to be addressed, as well as the disparity in hiring evident in the highest paying fields.

Backpage.com

Backpage.com has also been targeted by those seeking to stop sex trafficking. In 2015, Visa and MasterCard joined American Express in refusing to allow their credit cards to be used to purchase adult services ads on the site. While bitcoins can still be used for this purpose, this step will make it more difficult (Madhani, 2015).

Backpage.com has also faced lawsuits by those who were trafficked, alleging that the site facilitated their trafficking. A Boston judge threw out the lawsuit, stating that the site cannot be held responsible for the actions of its users (Madhani, 2015). However, the Washington Supreme Court ruled in favor of the plaintiffs, due to evidence that Backpage.com did not simply host the content but also helped develop the content by providing traffickers with instructions on how to write an ad that worked (Bellisle, 2015).

Improving Laws

Mentioned earlier, the Justice for Victims of Trafficking Act was passed in 2015 to address some of the gaps discussed in this book. This Act clarifies that domestic survivors are entitled to the same services as foreign survivors. It establishes a "Domestic Trafficking Victims' Fund," with the funding source being fines that are levied against buyers and exploiters. This fund will be used for grants for a variety of programs, including training, task forces, services, and court programs. It also increases available compensation and restitution available to survivors (as summarized by Shared Hope International, 2015).

The Bringing Missing Children Home Act, a portion of the larger Justice for Victims of Trafficking Act of 2015, P.L. 114-22, was enacted in May 2015. Among other improvements related to record-keeping, this legislation amended federal law to require that law enforcement agencies notify the National Center for Missing and Exploited Children (NCMEC) of each report they receive relating to a child missing from foster care. Additionally, the Preventing Sex Trafficking and Strengthening Families Act, P.L. 113-183 (H.R. 4980), enacted in September 2014, requires states to report every missing or abducted foster child to law enforcement and to NCMEC.

This addresses the reporting gap noted by Melissa Snow of NCMEC (interviewed in 2014). At the time of her interview, Ms. Snow advocated that all states should require caseworkers to report kids who go missing from foster care to NCMEC and not just their local law enforcement. NCMEC is a national entity that can work to locate a child regardless of what jurisdiction they are in and is dedicated to supporting the efforts of law enforcement to locate and recover missing and exploited children. Ms. Snow states:

[There are a lot of] resources that are available to people, that if it is a parent, legal guardian, law enforcement, whoever, for all missing kids, but obviously focusing on child sex trafficking specifically, that there is a specialized team, a child sex trafficking team here that has full-time analysts who work 24/7 and they have a huge amount of resources and access and specialty skills that law enforcement can call in and request assistance.

Anytime a kid is reported and identified as potentially a child sex trafficking victim, it goes to specialized teams that work to engage all resources at NCMEC. One of those resources includes the Child Sex Trafficking analytical team, and they employ a variety of different

analytical and specialized tools in addition to querying our own
internal systems to support the identification and recovery of that kid.
   Once a child is in our system, we never close a case until they are
found. There are long-term missing child cases on our radar and we
will not close a case until they are recovered alive or identified as
recovered deceased. This can be particularly helpful, especially with
so many kids being in state care because as they age out, all of that
knowledge that was with that social worker, once that case closes, they
can be the only person that had that knowledge and in some way had
them on their radar.

However, disappointingly, the bipartisan amendment to update services to runaway and homeless youth was not accepted to this bill. As
discussed in Chapter 1, these youth are at an extraordinarily high risk
of being trafficked. This is especially true for the disproportionately
large subset of LGBTQ youth within the population. This amendment
would have updated the Runaway and Homeless Youth and Trafficking
Prevention Act (RHYTPA) to strengthen current services, including
outreach and transitional living programs. It also would have explicitly
banned discrimination against LGBTQ youth (Human Rights Campaign,
2015; Polaris, 2015b).

State Laws

State-level laws are also an important tool to help address human trafficking. States have been working to improve their laws, and Polaris tracks
all 50 states to determine the quality of their laws regarding human trafficking. All 50 states now have a state-level law against human trafficking.
Even though the federal law has been in place since 2000, having these
state laws (as well as local laws) is a boon toward prosecution of these
facilitators. Special Agent Morlier states:

It helps when law enforcement agencies work together because
you have the flexibility to file local charges and the local systems are
geared toward dealing with a prisoner, an accused person within a
very short period of time. Filing the charges, establishing bail, and

determining probable cause all happen quickly. The federal system tends to move much slower and being able to file local charges to ensure the appearance of the accused is very important because there have been cases where the federal charges were substantiated, but by the time the federal system got going, the defendant had taken flight. And with trafficking, the defendants always want to take flight. There are always more customers, always more victims. Being able to charge something that night to either set a substantial bail or detain them, and then obtain the federal indictment with a potential more substantial sentence later, is an integral part of the effective system response.

Polaris assesses state laws in 10 categories to determine if the state has statutes in the areas listed below. Only three states—Delaware, New Jersey, and Washington—received perfect scores, indicating they had laws addressing all 10 areas. However, 39 states were in the top tier (Polaris, 2015c):

- Criminalize sex trafficking
- Criminalize labor trafficking
- Include legal tools, specifically:

  - Provide for asset forfeiture for earnings from human trafficking
  - Amend racketeering laws to include human trafficking

- Inform law enforcement by

  - Mandating or encouraging law enforcement training
  - Creating or encouraging anti–human trafficking task forces

- Mandate or encourage the posting of the Human Trafficking Hotline
- Provide survivors with the ability to seek civil damages
- Vacate prostitution convictions for sex trafficking survivors
- Create or support services for survivors

And specific to the topic of sex trafficking of minors:

- Ensure that force, fraud, and coercion are not required for prosecution of sex trafficking of a minor
- Have a "Safe Harbor" law

The passage of Safe Harbor laws has been a major area of advocacy for antitrafficking groups. Polaris (2014) describes a full Safe Harbor law as containing two aspects: legal protection and service provision. Legal protection provides minors with protection from prosecution for prostitution, by either immunity from prosecution or diversion from the criminal justice system. The services component recognizes that survivors need specialized services to heal from trafficking and requires that these services are offered. As of 2014, 15 states included both parts of the Safe Harbor law and 7 had one or the other (Polaris, 2014). Because fewer than half of the states offer any Safe Harbor protection, this clearly needs to be increased.

However, Safe Harbor laws, while overall positive, can have potential negative impacts due to other gaps in the system. If youth are arrested, they can move into the juvenile justice system and have a bed for the night. However, if they are not arrested, there is no emergency shelter for those who have been trafficked. Therefore, there is nowhere safe for the police or another agency to place them for the night. So this gap in policy needs to be addressed.

Some places follow the concept of Safe Harbor in practice, even when it is not law. For example, in Suffolk Country around Boston, even before the passage of the state Safe Harbor law, the district attorney declined to charge any minors because he recognized that they were victims of abuse, rather than perpetrators of crime. When they did update their law, it was required that any suspicion of domestic minor sex trafficking must be reported to their child welfare agency, just as any other case of suspected child abuse would be.

Changing the Way Systems Respond

It is not enough to just seat the right players at the table; they need to have the knowledge and ability to respond effectively. Training professionals about trafficking and changing systems to allow them to respond in an appropriate manner is a large part of being able to combat this crime effectively. Training must encompass overcoming stereotypes about prostituted youth—who they are and why they are there. Without training, there is a lack of knowledge as to what human trafficking is and how to recognize it. Although media awareness has been growing, the focus has typically been on only one type of survivor and one type of trafficker.

As discussed, this narrative that focuses on the pimp-controlled White girl who has been kidnapped and forced into slavery then inhibits the identification of others who are trafficked, including self-identification. Holly Austin Smith, survivor and author of *Walking Prey*, notes the lack of understanding that "willing victims" are also victims is harmful and leads to survivors questioning themselves if they were trafficked (Smith, 2015a). The knowledge that any child can be trafficked and physical force is not needed must be disseminated. Lisa Goldblatt Grace of My Life My Choice states that much of the awareness of trafficking and media attention:

---

is really wedded to images of women shackled to radiators and battered and bruised and from somewhere else. Or, if they're from the US, they're this innocent, preferably White, middle-class victim and the girls that we serve, some of them fit that profile for sure. But some of them have very complicated, challenging, painful histories that make it so that when you say, "I want to help," they say, "Go to hell." Which makes complete sense psychologically. But folks are still quick to say, "Well then, that's not a victim, let me go find the real ones," and that part is frustrating. So we're not really where we need to be yet.

Substantial progress has been made already in helping professionals understand what trafficking is. My Life My Choice does a lot of training of professionals, both service providers and law enforcement. Lisa Goldblatt Grace, director, notes the progress that has been made in understanding this crime over the years when she notes, "In the early days, the first half of the training, three quarters of the training might be spent just trying to convince folks that it's victimization, trying to get them to not make hooker jokes. And that doesn't happen anymore." However, work should continue to help them apply the knowledge from class to the field. Agent Morlier notes that for some police officers, they can accurately state what they learned in training, but they may not recognize cases in the field that are not clear-cut:

They know how to tell you what the instructor told them; this is human trafficking, this is what it looks like, this is what you do. But when they actually go out to enforce the law and they get called to an incident, if the incident is, for example, called in as a domestic dispute because people who see it just see people arguing, and they arrive and it ends up not being a husband/wife or girlfriend/boyfriend relationship, but clearly there's a relationship and clearly there's a power differential in the relationship and it ends up that the female is either a minor or a foreign national or has some sort of issue that would create that power differential, the light bulb doesn't go off, so to speak, that, well maybe this is something they were talking about in the class. It's treated as it's going to fit into one of the schemas that the officer already carries in their working knowledge. Is it domestic, is it an assault, is it a runaway? There's a lag between what they learn and when they start to apply it, and I think from what I read in some texts, there was the same problem with domestic violence several decades ago. There was a lag between the recognition that there needs to be change and when the officers on the street actually began to change.

The federal Administration for Children, Youth and Families agency (2013) notes that administrators must design their systems appropriately to deal with this issue. Their guidelines state that agencies must offer training on this issue to their staff, have appropriate policies and procedures, develop resources, and have appropriate screening tools for identification. If youth run away, agencies need to be prepared to respond appropriately when they return to determine if they were/are trafficked. They also state that coordination with other systems is essential, including agencies serving homeless youth and juvenile justice. The federal government is now changing its system by which it collects information on children who have been maltreated to collect information about children in the child welfare system who have been trafficked, either before entering, or while in, the foster care system (Department of Health and Human Services, 2015).

All those working in the child welfare system, whether as caseworkers, residential center staff, foster parents, or others, must be made aware of this issue and the red flags that may signal a child is being groomed or trafficked. They must also constantly work to meet a child's needs in a healthy way and ensure that the child feels accepted. As noted in Chapter 1, youth who do not identify as heterosexual are especially vulnerable to maltreatment and rejection *within* the child welfare system, which then causes them to be at higher risk of being trafficked. Dank (2013) states that in order to reduce trafficking, child welfare systems must address problems within their own systems, including increasing the following: caseworker stability, access to mental health services, training for foster parents, and peer-led groups.

Due to the busy schedules of child welfare staff, statewide training can be difficult to schedule. Therefore, Georgia developed a webinar to address this need. The webinar was designed to increase knowledge in identifying child sex trafficking as well as its scope and demand, risk factors for becoming trafficked, indicators that someone is trafficked, and screening questions to use with youth. When assessing participants' knowledge 3 months later, those who participated in the training were significantly more knowledgeable than they themselves had been before the training and as compared to those who had not received the training (McMahon-Howard & Reimers, 2013).

State laws also need to be changed to allow these children access to services. Many states limit the definition of child abuse to a person who is that child's guardian, which means that children who have been trafficked by a non–family member cannot be placed in a foster home or residential treatment center and receive services provided to children in the custody of the child welfare system. The only option available for law enforcement then is the juvenile justice system, thus labeling the child as a criminal, and which may not be available if Safe Harbor laws are in place. Melissa Snow of the NCMEC tells the following story:

I was talking with a law enforcement officer the other day, actually reviewing the child welfare law, and in that state the child welfare law, as it was currently written, would not allow the child survivor of sex trafficking being controlled by a nonfamilial trafficker to be eligible for accessing services from the child welfare system. It required the first responder to advocate significantly and really make a solid argument that the trafficker had become the "caregiver" in this child's life. It was painfully obvious the law had not been updated to include child sex trafficking or any type of nonfamilial exploiter in a child sex trafficking situation to be a scenario in which child welfare should be involved. And so for this law enforcement officer who desperately wanted this child to get what the services she needed as a victim of a crime, the only

option that he had was to put her in some form of juvenile detention
facility because the law didn't allow him to go another direction.

———————

She continues on to discuss how this can be an even bigger issue if
the child is recovered in a state different from the one in which the child
lives, a common occurrence:

———————

So we need to continue having conversations about systems
change. Not expecting that either kids know how to navigate
these complicated systems or that they're going to have the proper
advocates within these systems that are going to say, "No, this is
inappropriate" or "This kid should go this way." In order for a
survivor of trafficking to access immediate and appropriate services,
systems, communities and professionals need to adjust their current
laws, policies, and perceptions. A survivor's access to services, and
being viewed as a victim with rights, should not depend on one
well-intended person or advocate. What happens when that person
is not there? These victim-centered and informed responses must be
integrated into the psyche and the core of our response and service
systems.

———————

Systems must also share information in order to identify and assist survivors to leave the life. Tesy Molina of Multicultural Counseling Center
notes that she encountered her first known trafficking survivor when she
was working as a probation officer. She asked a local agency to complete
an assessment to determine formally whether she had been trafficked;
they complied and confirmed that she was, but they refused to share a
copy of the assessment, which inhibited Ms. Molina from connecting the
survivor with appropriate services.

Ideally, systems will work together to address this crime, and multidisciplinary teams have been identified as a vital tool to facilitate this. An
area assessed by Polaris as essential in fighting human trafficking is the
use of task forces. Melissa Snow of NCMEC notes that communities that
utilize multidisciplinary task forces have been very effective in helping

to fight this crime. The use of task forces often creates opportunities for more information sharing, more training, and more awareness of other parts of the system that can be helpful in identification and response.

In Boston, reports of potential trafficking are sent to the antitrafficking multidisciplinary team known as the Support to End Exploitation (SEEN) coalition. Donna Gavin, lieutenant in the Boston Police Department and the commander of the Human Trafficking Unit, states the formation of the unit in 2005 was due to the unsolved murder of a 17-year-old in Bedford, Massachusetts, who had entered the child protection services system in Boston when she was 16. She seemed to have fallen through the cracks of the system, and the coalition was formed to prevent the same occurrence for other youth. Gavin recalls:

[Before the formation of the coalition], you'd be called out in the Sexual Assault Unit to an emergency room where there was a teenager. You know, she's there, obviously traumatized, she's not telling you what's going on though, at that point you just had to move on to the next case. People started realizing there's something going on here and that's how the unit was started. Nationally there were federal grants given out to start task forces and BPD was awarded one of them.

In Boston, they have colocated the Human Trafficking Unit of the police department, the Child Advocacy Center staff who work with those who have been trafficked, and the NGO My Life My Choice that assists in the psychological recovery process. This collaboration has created a more seamless approach to assisting those who have been trafficked. These parties all participate in the multidisciplinary SEEN coalition.

The SEEN coalition has been very effective in coordinating a broad spectrum of professionals when a referral of a possible case of sexual exploitation of a child is received. Beth Bouchard, the program manager for the state, will receive that referral, identify the people who need to be involved, and pull them together to staff the case and coordinate the response. The SEEN coalition exemplifies the concept of a multidisciplinary team because of this broad spectrum of those who may be involved. Ms. Bouchard notes the following as those who may be involved in a case:

The Massachusetts Department of Children and Families; the Suffolk County District Attorney's Office; Probation; the Department of Youth Services; exploitation-specific support service providers, including Life Coaches from the GIFT Program or Mentors from My Life My Choice; the Boston Police Department Human Trafficking Unit; the juvenile defense bar; mental health and therapeutic support service providers; medical providers; residential placement providers; and other collaterals who interface with youth.

Having a full-time case coordinator makes a huge difference to the efficiency and effectiveness of the multi-disciplinary team. Ms. Bouchard not only identifies the needed players for each case and coordinates the meeting, but she also gathers the history on the case, follows the person as the case proceeds, and updates the team on progress. She schedules interviews and makes referrals as appropriate, such as to My Life My Choice.

In another example of interdisciplinary collaboration, working across unexpected partners has shown huge results. Polaris runs the national trafficking hotline. When survivors called, the call specialists were spending valuable time locating the survivors on a map, and then paging through a huge list of protocols and resources to find the appropriate information. Palantir Technologies, a data analysis firm, stepped in and created software that allows the call specialist to essentially click a button and information on how to respond in that area will appear. It also allows the specialist to account for such variables as age, immigration status, and shelter needs. Second, by gathering all these data, analysis can be conducted, allowing trends to be spotted and Polaris to move from only responding to being better able to be proactive in outreach and prevention (Sneed, 2015).

Appropriate Services and Outreach

As discussed, services specific to this crime are needed, as well as specific to the type of trafficking and type of survivor. As described earlier in this chapter, while Safe Harbor laws are overall very positive, due to how systems function, an unintended consequence has been reducing the availability of emergency beds for those recovered from trafficking situations as juvenile justice beds are no longer an option. Law enforcement officers may encounter someone who does want to leave, but they may have nowhere to put that person for the night. Long-term housing is also a need. Residential services are still limited overall, and there are even fewer beds and other services for boys or trans* youth.

As detailed in Chapter 4, requirements for quality in residential services need to be established. As Ms. Frundt stated, a federal standard of care needs to be developed, as has been done for domestic violence shelters. Additionally, these providers need to ensure they are deeply informed about the methods and impacts of trafficking, or they may be further harming survivors. For example, some of these shelters have mandatory religious requirements for residents, which can be harmful for those who were bought by religious leaders or felt abandoned by their faith. In other cases, unwitting staff have placed rival gang members in the same shelter.

In the previous chapter, it was discussed that the voice of survivors is seen as essential by many of those providing services; many agencies are survivor run, utilize survivor-mentors, and guide their services on that survivor voice. This empowerment of survivors aids in their recovery, and it helps others recover as well. However, this voice has been identified as lacking in many media messages—both in outreach to those who are being trafficked and those to raise public awareness. Holly Austin Smith (2015b), herself a survivor, notes that women are frequently dehumanized in antitrafficking images. They are depicted as products, perhaps even with a UPC code on their body, and as unable to speak for themselves, such as with tape or others' hands over their mouths. Because survivors, including Ms. Smith, have experienced being sensationalized for their experiences and valued only as victims, this perpetuates the concept of them as passive. Ms. Smith calls on us to consider the images we use and what message they send about those who are trafficked—Are they human beings or are they objects for sale? Rebecca Bender (2013), a survivor leader, encourages other survivors to watch for re-exploitation, such as by the media in which survivors are used for their story. She stated she will be asked to drive hours to speak for free at an event by a group—thus once again being asked to labor without compensation.

Ms. Smith also analyzes whether or not outreach posters are likely to reach survivors with their message—both in pictures or words. She notes that those who are being trafficked must be able to identify themselves as the target audience if they are to be effective. She notes one poster as having an effective picture but its words, "Is someone controlling you?"—are a message to which many trafficked youth will not relate. As described in this text, many youth are either not under the control of a third person or do not identify themselves as being controlled. She commends Alameda County as well as Truckers Against Trafficking for getting feedback from survivors to design their outreach posters and using quotes from actual survivors to make it more likely those in the life will identify with them (Smith, 2015c).

At My Life My Choice, survivors have developed pamphlets for child protective services and residential centers with basic messages such as "Has this ever happened to you because it happened to us and this is how we got out" or "We've been right where you are; this is what we felt at the time and here's how we got to a place of feeling hopeful." They also worked with a photojournalist to create an exhibit about their experiences that has been displayed in various places to educate people about trafficking.

Prevention

To truly address trafficking, we need to look at the drivers of it—not only for the exploiters, but for the survivors. This requires a focus on the risk factors described in Chapter 1 and addressing the vulnerabilities they create. It is necessary to focus on deleterious childhood experiences. As Minh Dang states, whose story of familial trafficking was shared in Chapter 2, a focus on buyers is too narrow:

I think we're missing a crucial piece here, which is that these kids are being abused most likely at home, and in my experience being sold by their own parents, whether directly or given by their parents to other people to sell. And so focusing on the johns is really kind of a symptom, rather than focusing on whether the kids are running away from an abusive home. (Chan, 2013, para. 13)

When considering prevention, both societal and personal factors must be addressed. When looking at personal factors, prevention on all levels is important: primary, secondary, and tertiary. In conducting secondary prevention, one intervention that may assist in the prevention of trafficking for those who have experienced child maltreatment utilizes a risk detection/executive function approach. It focuses on teaching clients how to recognize cues of potential victimization and methods of responding to those cues. This aligns well with the information in Chapter 1 about the impact of trauma on the brain which noted that trauma can result in difficulties understanding and regulating emotion, underdeveloped empathetic abilities, increased aggression, and an increase in impulsivity (Reid & Jones, 2011). In a longitudinal study with adolescent girls in the child welfare system, those who received this intervention were five times less likely to be revictimized than those in the control group (DePrince, Chu, Labus, Shirk, & Potter, 2015).

My Life My Choice in Boston has created a gender-specific prevention program for the girls considered to be at highest risk for being trafficked. Lisa Goldblatt Grace, director, notes that many prevention programs are being developed to increase awareness, but in order to be as effective as possible with this population, this is insufficient. As noted in Chapter 1, knowledge is insufficient to dissuade teens from risky actions (Arden & Linford, 2009). She reflects on her experience with HIV prevention, in which she found that simply educating youth about the risks did not lower their likelihood of infection. She looked at the evidence base of the help belief model, which states that in order to shift behavior, attitudes, knowledge, and skills must all be a target. My Life My Choice has been training people from all over the country in this model for them to utilize in their own area. The groups are co-led by a survivor and a mental health professional. In conducting these groups, she has found that "We almost have never done a group that we haven't had disclosures, that girls haven't said, 'I never told anybody this before, I never had the language to talk about it before, it's happened to me or my sister or my mom.'"

However, conducting primary prevention programs can be very difficult. The ability of groups to access schools can be difficult due to concerns about anything involving the word "sex." Thus, parents need to make sure they are accurately informed about trafficking and take steps to protect their children. Tina Frundt of Courtney's House encourages parents to have frank discussions with their children about trafficking—what it is, how recruiters behave, and so forth. She states that the most essential thing is for parents to know what their child does on a daily basis and to monitor their child's Internet activity. She states that it is worrisome "if you don't know their password to the Internet, because the pimp could be in your house right now. How do you know who they're talking to?" (Pierce, 2015, para. 18). As noted by Special Agent Morlier in Chapter 1, many parents are becoming aware of the need to monitor computer activity, but this should include cell phone activity as well, including chat apps. Secondary prevention, focusing on groups at higher risk, can be easier because conducting programs in foster care group homes or juvenile justice facilities can actually be easier, according to Lisa Goldblatt Grace.

As discussed in Chapter 1, there are a number of societal issues that place some people at higher risk of being trafficked, such as child abuse, poverty, racism, heterosexism, and the sexualization of girls. Several providers discussed the need to address these broader issues in order to address trafficking effectively. None of these are easy issues, and it will take a societal-wide effort to chip away at these driving issues, but if we are truly committed to stopping this crime, our efforts need to include a focus on why it occurs in the first place. Society is moving from thinking of these children as criminals to understanding them as crime victims. To continue to progress, we need to address these issues that can create vulnerability. Although they may seem huge and intractable, they are not unsolvable. As one example, the rate of child abuse has dropped markedly in recent decades (Finkelhor & Jones, 2006), showing us that such issues can be addressed.

Julie Laurence at GEMS states:

We always talk about trafficking in the larger system view; that this isn't just happening because there are people who are buying and selling them, but it's happening because of economic injustice. So we need to look at poverty, look at the mass incarceration of people of color, look at the ongoing patriarchal system that doesn't value women and girls on the same level. All of those things contribute to a society where people are vulnerable and marginalized. So we need to really try to address those issues as well, and include racism and sexism and all the big-ticket items that really need to be addressed in order to live in a society that's equal and fair.

Her colleague Jessica Trudeau notes that looking at broader systems of service provision is important when looking at both prevention and recovery. This can include housing systems, employment, and child care, "all those things that low-income people of color are denied in the first place and they're denied on the other end as well."

To reach those who are at highest risk, we must disregard media stereotypes. If we are only looking for the White suburban girl who has been kidnapped and physically forced or coerced, we will not see the vast majority of those who have been trafficked. If we do not address the root vulnerabilities, we will not stop trafficking. Amelia Rubenstein states:

When I see ads for the Slave Hunter, I want to cry. Because this whole rescue complex does not help anyone. It hurts everyone. Someone said, "Rescue is for kittens" and that's so, so true. Because there's groups of people who are like, "Oh, I really want to help trafficking survivors, but I do not want to give food stamps to people in poverty."

There are things that are very, very unique about trafficking survivors. So how can we take what's already being created and try to make sure that it's working for them too. Because usually these are the kids who have fallen through all those other systems. So can we work on fixing these systems?

I ask survivors, "What would have helped you tell somebody or reach out sooner?" And they always say, "I didn't even know that there was help for this." They all know that there's help for domestic violence. Sometimes they know that there's help for sexual assault. Maybe they stayed in a domestic violence shelter with their mom when they were little. So they know that that's kind of out there, but the idea that there's help for this is not even on their radar. And so I think we just have to make sure this is an issue we are talking to kids about just like everything else, healthy relationships, sexual health, etc., that we talk to them about.

Conclusion

Thus, there is much work that needs to be done. Much of this works needs to be done by the professionals that society has appointed to it—law enforcement, social workers, social service professionals, and so forth. However, there is a great deal that everyday people—students, church members, Rotary Clubs, whoever has the passion—can accomplish if oriented in the right direction. This is discussed in the final chapter.

6

Conclusion

The awareness of domestic minor sexual trafficking is growing, both among professionals and the community, which has had positive impacts in a variety of ways. Increased community awareness has led to more youth being identified as being trafficked, which helps connect them to services. Community awareness of the nature and impacts of trafficking also helps reduce cultural tolerance for purchasing people for sex (Shared Hope International, 2015). Increased awareness, stronger laws, and stronger enforcement of those laws also appear to be affecting the rate of this crime. Law enforcement in several cities noted that pimps are now less interested in recruiting those under 18; pimps know they will be easy to prosecute in these cases because force, fraud, and coercion do not need to be proven for children under 18.

However, this leads to an important note. There is a lot of sympathy for those who are under 18 and are involved in the sex trade, but not for those who are over 18. As discussed, many of those over 18 were brought in when they were younger and now do not believe they can do anything else. Also, one provider stated that their statistics showed a spike of entry at age 18, which she believed was related to the fact that these youth are no longer eligible for many services and become homeless. The risk factors discussed in Chapter 1 do not suddenly ameliorate on one's 18th birthday, and the loss of services can make matters even worse. Corporal Chris Heid of the Maryland State Police states, "If we could get the stiffer penalties, that if you pimp anybody under the age of 21, it's a felony, I think we'd have the same impact as we're having with the juveniles."

There needs to be a shift in societal attitude to allow those who would like to leave the sex trade the ability to do so. One model that has been found to be effective originated in Sweden, where the selling of sex is not illegal, but the purchase of it is. This helps address the demand factor in the sex trade. A 2010 evaluation of the law found that street prostitution had been reduced by half, while in contrast it grew dramatically in Norway and Denmark—neighboring countries without such a law. Internet prostitution did grow in Sweden, but not as extensively as in Norway and Denmark. Thus, there was not support for the concern that the law would merely move prostitution. It appears to have led to an actual decrease in demand (Swedish Institute, 2010). Swedish police and social workers report that criminal groups involved in prostitution regard Sweden as a "poor market" and avoid it due to this law. Other countries, including Norway, Iceland, and Ireland, have now adopted their own version of the law (Ask, 2011).

As noted, media images and stories, supported by some organizations, have created the idea that there is one type of trafficking and one type of person who is trafficked. Many providers noted the broad range of types of clients with whom they worked, and they emphasized that anyone can be trafficked, regardless of age, sex, gender, class, race, sexual orientation, or any other demographic category. The image of the White suburban girl who is tricked or kidnapped and then held by force is harmful to identifying trafficking, both by others and by the survivor themselves.

The long, difficult road to healing needs to be understood by both the survivor and the community. Undoing the ravages of complex trauma is not simple work, nor is it short-term work, and the therapy involved requires highly skilled clinicians. For professionals who are seeking resources, Courtney's House in Washington, DC, sells their model to other agencies seeking to improve their services. My Life My Choice conducts training for professionals, as discussed, but also provides trainings for those wishing to use their curriculum, as well as offers program and case consultation.

What Can I Do?

Although there is much work for professionals to do, there is also a role for the everyday citizen. But this must be done in a thoughtful way, so as

not to create further harm. Many of those working in the field emphasized that those wishing to help fight trafficking should not just jump in
and start an agency or a campaign. There are many good existing agencies
and programs that need support, and further splitting the attention and
the funding does not serve the cause, but weakens it. There is grave concern about people/groups who read a book or see a news piece and then
want to start an organization. Those interviewed emphasize that this is
difficult and complex work and going into it with no background will do
further harm to those who have been trafficked.

This sentiment has been echoed by survivors. Holly Austin Smith
(2014, p. 170) states that when asked what everyday people can do to
help prevent the sexual exploitation of children, her number-one answer
is *"Support services in your community!"* (emphasis original). Minh Dang
(Chan, 2013, para. 23) states, "Please just read and learn more before
taking action." This includes the broader picture of trafficking, including
both labor trafficking and sex trafficking, to understand the diversity of
experiences. Ms. Dang also notes the importance of people first addressing any trauma and abuse they themselves have suffered before seeking to
help others. She adds that given the known high rates of child sexual abuse
in the United States, it is important for people to create space in their personal relationships for people to disclose what has occurred to them.

Once people are ready to volunteer with an agency, there are a variety of paths they can follow. The following suggestions are taken from
the interviews conducted for this book, together with those from Minh
Dang (Chan, 2013) and Holly Austin Smith (2014). Dang states, "Try to
use your skills and knowledge in your area of expertise, and do what you
love . . . like, if you like baking or making jewelry. Build it into your life in
a way that's sustainable, rather than adding some new crusade to go on."

As discussed by many of the professionals interviewed, human trafficking is an issue that is rooted in various forms of societal oppression: poverty, sexism, heterosexism, educational inequality, and racism. If you focus
on any of those, you will be helping the antitrafficking cause. An agency
does not need to address trafficking specifically to help. You can:

- Join with a nonprofit that is already doing the work, because
  they have been in the field and have avenues for you to get
  involved. These include:
  - fundraising
  - donating

- becoming a mentor
- raising awareness
- organizing a drive for a nonprofit's wish list
- organizing a documentary screening
- Be a mentor to a child
- Be a tutor at an underfunded school
- Be a foster parent
- Volunteer at an agency that assists those who are:
  - homeless
  - battling substance abuse
  - impoverished
  - sexual minorities
  - at risk for committing/experiencing abuse/neglect
  - at risk for dropping out of school
  - being bullied
  - struggling with mental health issues

Some agencies use mentors to create positive role models for survivors working on their healing journey. As noted, mentors who are themselves survivors offer a role model that it is possible to get out on the other side, but others, if well trained, can assist as well. The training is necessary to make sure the mentors, however well intentioned, do not delay the healing journey. For example, a mentor may want to buy gifts for the mentee, but as Lisa Dingle of Youth For Tomorrow notes, "They've become accustomed to that; their relationship with their pimps was based on exchange of goods, without a relationship," and therefore it can be important to curb this impulse. She adds that protocols and processes for mentor programs are also important because it is necessary to assess if the mentor is ready because otherwise the mentor may be traumatized by the survivor's story. Mentors may have experienced trauma themselves, and this can cause it to resurface. Also, if mentors are not ready to hear the youth's stories and accept them in a nonjudgmental way, including not being horrified for the youth, the mentor's reaction can damage the youth's healing.

Many agencies use only survivor mentors for their clients, but for those who are interested in being a mentor, Julie Laurence of GEMS encourages them to work with other agencies, such as Big Brothers, Big Sisters, which serve those youth at higher risk for being trafficked. She notes that we know that if the youth have stable, healthy adults in their life, they are less likely to be trafficked.

Conclusion

The state of knowledge about domestic minor sex trafficking continues to evolve—what it is, why it occurs, and what can be done about it. This book offers information gathered primarily from scholarly articles or directly from professionals working with survivors, together with information from the news, in an attempt to dispel the myths and stereotypes about this crime that hinder addressing it effectively. The amount of respect that should be given to these providers cannot be overstated. They are working to help children recover from some of the most horrific experiences that a person can have—day in and day out. Yet uniformly they were hopeful about their work and passionate about what they do. They were also deeply impressed with the youth with whom they worked. They honored the strength it took to even come to their attention and the greater strength to do the hard work of healing from trauma. May this book aid in this work.

List of Participants

Beth Bouchard
SEEN Program Manager
Children's Advocacy
    Center of Suffolk County
Boston, MA
Interviewed May 2, 2013

Megan Caesar, MA
Therapist
Youth For Tomorrow
Bristow, VA
Interviewed January 7, 2014

Lisa Dingle, MA
Therapist
Youth For Tomorrow
Bristow, VA
Interviewed January 7, 2014

Connie Espino
Field Probation Officer
E.S.T.E.E.M. Court;
    Dallas County Juvenile
    Department
Dallas, TX
Located at Letot Center
Interviewed November 1, 2013

Tina Frundt
Executive Director and Founder
Courtney's House
United States Advisory Board on
    Human Trafficking, appointee
Washington, DC
Interviewed May 5, 2014

Donna Gavin, JD
Lieutenant
Commander of the Human
    Trafficking Unit
Boston Police Department
Boston, MA
Interviewed May 2, 2013

Lisa Goldblatt Grace, LICSW, MPH
Co-Founder & Director
My Life My Choice
Boston, MA
Interviewed May 2, 2013

Chris Heid
Corporal
Child Recovery Unit
Maryland State Police
Columbia, MD
Interviewed January 24, 2014

Julie Laurence, LMSW
Chief Program Officer
GEMS
New York, NY
Interviewed June 8, 2015

Bonnie Martin, LPC
Psychotherapist, Educator,
   Consultant
Alexandria, VA
Interviewed March 4, 2014

Tesy Molina, BA, QMHP
Intensive Home-Based Counselor
Multicultural Clinical Center
Springfield, VA
Interviewed March 7, 2014

Louis Morlier, MSW
Special Agent
Department of Homeland
   Security
Middletown, PA
Interviewed March 22, 2013

Deepa Patel, CSOTP, LCSW
Clinical Consultant on Gangs and
   Trafficking Gang Intervention
   and Sexual Exploitation
   Program Director Sex Offender
   Program Coordinator
Multicultural Clinical Center
 Springfield, VA
Interviewed January 7, 2014

Amelia Rubenstein, LCSW-C
Team Leader
Anti-Trafficking Program
Turnaround, Inc.
Baltimore, MD
Interviewed January 24, 2014

Melissa Snow, MA
Program Specialist on Child Sex
   Trafficking
National Center for Missing and
   Exploited Children
Alexandria, VA
Interviewed January 6, 2014

Jessica Trudeau, MPH
Program Director
GEMS
New York, NY
Interviewed June 8, 2015

Resources

Websites

Polaris: www.polarisproject.com
An excellent go-to source with a plethora of information about all forms of trafficking, including state-level information. They run the National Human Trafficking Hotline, and you can locate local agencies on their website.

Books

Institute of Medicine and National Research Council. (2013). *Confronting commercial sexual exploitation and sex trafficking of minors in the United States.* Washington, DC: National Academic Press.

Lloyd, R. (2011). *Girls like us.* New York, NY: HarperCollins.

Malarek, V. (2011). *The johns: Sex for sale and the men who buy it.* New York, NY: Arcade.

Sheer, J. (2011). *Somebody's daughter: The hidden story of America's prostituted children and the battle to save them.* Chicago, IL: Chicago Review.

Smith, H. (2014). *Walking prey: How America's youth are vulnerable to sex slavery.* New York, NY: Palgrave Macmillan.

Therapeutic Approach Resources

Briere, J. N., & Lanktree, C. B. (2012). *Treating complex trauma in adolescents and young adults*. Thousand Oaks, CA: Sage.

Briere, J. N., & Scott, C. (2013). *Principles of trauma therapy: A guide to symptoms, evaluation and treatment* (2nd ed.). Thousand Oaks, CA: Sage.

Cohen, J. A., Mannarino, A. P., & Deblinger, E. (2006). *Treating trauma and traumatic grief in children and adolescents*. New York, NY: Guilford.

Ford, J. D., & Courtois, C. A. (2013). *Treating complex traumatic stress disorders in children and adolescents: Scientific foundations and therapeutic models*. New York, NY: Guilford.

Online TF-CBT training for therapists: http://www.musc.edu/tfcbt

References

Administration for Children, Youth, and Families. (2013). *Guidance to states and services on addressing human trafficking of children and youth in the United States.* Retreived from http://www.acf.hhs.gov/programs/cb/resource/human-trafficking-guidance

Allen, E. (2010). *Testimony before the House subcommittee on crime, terrorism and homeland security.* Retrieved from http://www.gpo.gov/fdsys/pkg/CHRG-111hhrg58250/html/CHRG-111hhrg58250.htm

Alter, C. (2014, August 5). Cops arrest 500 johns in sex trade crackdown. *Time.* Retrieved from http://time.com/3083244/sex-trafficking-prostitution-national-day-of-johns-arrests/

American Psychological Association Task Force on the Sexualization of Girls. (2007). *Report of the APA Task Force on the Sexualization of Girls.* Retrieved from http://www.apa.org/pi/women/programs/girls/report.aspx

Annitto, M. (2011). Consent, coercion, and compassion: Emerging legal responses to the commercial sexual exploitation of minors. *Yale Law and Policy Review, 30*(1), 1–70.

Applegate, J. S., & Shapiro, J. R. (2005). *Neurobiology for clinical social work: Theory and practice.* New York, NY: Norton.

Arden, J. B., & Linford, L. (2009). *Brain-based therapy with children and adolescents: Evidence-based treatment for everyday practice.* Hoboken, NJ: Wiley.

Ashley, J. (2008). *The commercial sexual exploitation of children and youth in Illinois.* Retrieved from http://www.icjia.state.il.us/public/pdf/researchreports/ csec%202008%20icjia%20report.pdf

Ask, B. (2011, March 31). Sweden: Why we criminalized purchase of sexual services. *CNN.* Retrieved from http://www.cnn.com/2011/OPINION/03/31/sweden.beatrice.ask.trafficking/

Bales, K., & Lize, S. (2005). *Trafficking in persons in the United States: A report to the National Institute of Justice.* Retrieved from https://www.ncjrs.gov/pdffiles1/nij/grants/211980.pdf

Beck, M. E., Lineer, M. M., Melzer-Lange, M., Simpson, P., Nugent, M., & Rabbitt, A. (2015). Medical providers' understanding of sex trafficking and their experience with at-risk patients. *Pediatrics, 135*(4), e895–e902.

Bellisle, M. (2015, September 3). Washington Supreme Court rules against Backpage.com. *AP.* Retrieved from http://bigstory.ap.org/article/4b231e3c058e41fe8492562bc523fc7a/washington-supreme-court-rules-against-backpagecom

Bender, R. (2013, November). *Inside the mind of a victim.* Paper presented at Shared Hope International's JuST (Juvenile Sex Trafficking) Conference, Washington, DC.

Betancourt, T. S., Newnham, E. A., McBain, R., & Brennan, R. T. (2013). Post-traumatic stress symptoms among former child soldiers in Sierra Leone: Follow-up study. *British Journal of Psychiatry, 203,* 196–202.

Betancourt, T. S., Borisova, I., Williams, T. P., Meyers-Ohki, S. E., Rubin-Smith, J. E., Annan, J., & Kohrt, B. A. (2013). Research review: Psychosocial adjustment and mental health in former child soldiers- a systematic review of the literature and recommendations for future research. *Journal of Child Psychology and Psychiatry, 54*(1), 17–36.

Beyer, M. (2011). A developmental view of youth in the juvenile justice system. In F. T. Sherman & F. H. Jacobs (Eds.), *Juvenile justice: Advancing research, policy, and practice* (pp. 3–23). Hoboken, NJ: Wiley.

Blakemore, S., & Robbins, T. W. (2012). Decision-making in the adolescent brain. *Nature Neuroscience, 15*(9), 1184–1191.

Brawn, K. M., & Roe-Sepowitz, D. (2008). Female juvenile prostitutes: Exploring the relationship to substance use. *Children and Youth Services Review, 30,* 1395–1402.

Briere, J. N., & Lanktree, C. B. (2012). *Treating complex trauma in adolescents and young adults.* Thousand Oaks, CA: Sage.

Briere, J., & Scott, C.. (2013). *Principles of trauma therapy: A guide to symptoms, evaluation and treatment* (2nd ed.). Thousand Oaks, CA: Sage.

Burque, A. D. (2009). *Empowering young men to end sexual exploitation.* Retrieved from http://media.virbcdn.com/files/54/FileItem-149405-CAASEcurriculum1_19.pdf

Centers for Disease Control and Prevention. (2014). *Major findings*. Retrieved from http://www.cdc.gov/violenceprevention/acestudy/findings.html

Chan, B. (2013, June 3). Minh Dang on fighting modern-day slavery in Bay Area and worldwide. *Oakland Local*. Retrieved from http://oaklandlocal.com/2013/06/minh-dang-on-fighting-modern-day-slavery-in-oakland-and-world-wide/

Chang, K. S. G., Lee, K., Park, T., Sy, E., & Quach, T. (2015). Using a clinic-based screening tool for primary care providers to identify commercially sexually exploited children. *Journal of Applied Research on Children*, 6(1), Article 6. Retrieved from http://digitalcommons.library.tmc.edu/cgi/viewcontent.cgi?article=1235&context=childrenatrisk /

Children's Bureau. (2014). *AFCARS report #21*. Retrieved from http://www.acf.hhs.gov/programs/cb/resource/afcars-report-21

Clarke, R. J., Clarke, E. A. Roe-Sepowitz, D., & Fey, R. (2012). Age at entry into prostitution: Relationship to drug use, race, suicide, education level, childhood abuse, and family experiences. *Journal of Human Behavior in the Social Environment*, 22, 270–289.

Clawson, H. J., & Goldblatt Grace, L. (2007). *Finding a path to recovery: Residential facilities for minor victims of domestic sex trafficking*. Retrieved from http://aspe.hhs.gov/hsp/07/humantrafficking/ResFac/ib.htm

Clawson, H. J., Salomon, A., & Goldblatt Grace, L. (2008). Treating the hidden wounds: Trauma treatment and mental health recovery for victims of human trafficking. *US Department of Health and Human Services*. Retrieved from http://aspe.hhs.gov/hsp/07/humantrafficking/Treating/ib.htm

Clements, J. A., & Rosenwald, M. (2007). Foster parents' perspectives on LGB youth in the child welfare system. *Journal of Gay and Lesbian Social Services*, 19(1), 57–69. doi:10.1300/J041v19n01_04

Cohen, J. A., Mannarino, A. P., & Deblinger, E. (2006). *Treating trauma and traumatic grief in children and adolescents*. New York, NY: Guilford Press.

Colby, I. (2011). Runaway and throwaway youth: Time for policy changes and public responsibility. *Journal of Applied Research on Children*, 2(1). Retrieved from http://digitalcommons.library.tmc.edu/childrenatrisk/vol2/iss1/4/

Cole, J., & Anderson, E. (2013). *Sex trafficking of minors in Kentucky*. Retrieved from http://uknowledge.uky.edu/ctac_reports/2

Cole, J., & Sprang, G. (2015). Sex trafficking of minors in metropolitan, micropolitan, and rural communities. *Child Abuse & Neglect*, 40, 113–123.

Cook, A., Spinazzola, J., Ford, J., Lanktree, C., Blaustein, M., Cloitre, M., ... van der Kolk, B. (2005). Complex trauma in children and adolescents. *Psychiatric Annals*, 35(5), 390–398.

Courtney, M. E., Skyles, A., Miranda, G., Zinn, A., Howard, E., & Goerge, R. M. (2005a). *Youth who run away from out-of-home care*. Retrieved from http://www.chapinhall.org/research/brief/youth-who-run-away-out-home-care

Courtney, M. E., Skyles, A., Miranda, G., Zinn, A., Howard, E., & Goerge, R. M. (2005b). *Youth who run away from substitute care*. Retrieved from http://www.chapinhall.org/research/report/youth-who-run-away-substitute-care

Covenant House. (2013). *Homelessness, survival sex and human trafficking: As experienced by the youth of Covenant House New York*. Retrieved from http://center.serve.org/nche/downloads/cov-hs-trafficking.pdf

Coy, M. (2009). "Moved around like bags of rubbish nobody wants": How multiple placement moves can make young women vulnerable to sexual exploitation. *Child Abuse Review, 18*, 254–266. doi:10.1002/car.1064

Coy, M., Wakeling, J., & Garner, M. (2011). Selling sex sells: Representations of prostitution and the sex industry in sexualised popular culture as symbolic violence. *Women's Studies International Forum, 34*, 441–448.

Craven, S., Brown, S., & Gilchrist, E. (2006). Sexual grooming of children: Review of literature and theoretical considerations. *Journal of Sexual Aggression, 12*(3), 287–299. doi:10.1080/13552600601069414

D'Amico, E. (2014). Trauma and stress: Neural networks. In H. C. Johnson (Ed.), *Behavioral neuroscience for the human services* (pp. 144–165). New York, NY: Oxford University Press.

Dank, M. (2013). *Four steps for keeping at-risk youth from engaging in the sex trade*. Retrieved from http://www.urban.org/urban-wire/four-steps-keeping-risk-youth-engaging-sex-trade

Dank, M., Khan, B., Downey, P. M., Kotonias, C., Mayer, D., Owens, C., . . . Yu, L. (2014). *Estimating the size and structure of the underground commercial sex economy in eight major US cities*. Retrieved from http://www.urban.org/UploadedPDF/413047-Underground-Commercial-Sex-Economy.pdf

Dank, M., Yahner, J., Madden, K., Bañuelos, I., Yu, L., Ritchie, A., . . . Conner, B. (2015). *Surviving the streets of New York: Experiences of LGBTQ youth, YMSM, and YWSW engaged in survival sex*. Retrieved from http://www.urban.org/research/publication/surviving-streets-new-york-experiences-lgbtq-youth-ymsm-and-ywsw-engaged-survival-sex

Dank, M. L. (2011). *The commercial sexual exploitation of children*. El Paso, TX: LFB Scholarly.

de Carvalho, H. W., Pereira, R., Frozi, J., Bisol, L. W., Ottoni, G. L., & Lara, D. R. (2015). Childhood trauma is associated with maladaptive personality traits. *Child Abuse & Neglect, 44*, 18–25.

Demand Abolition. (n.d.a). *CEASE network in action*. Retrieved from https://www.demandabolition.org/blog/cease-network-in-action

Demand Abolition. (n.d.b). *Washington state communities unite to reduce demand for commercial sexual exploitation*. Retrieved from https://www.demandabolition.org/blog/seattle-reduce-demand

Dennis, J. P. (2008). Women are victims, men make choices: The invisibility of men and boys in the global sex trade. *Gender Issues, 25*, 11–25. doi:10.1007/s12147-008-9051-y

DePrince, A. P., Chu, A. T., Labus, J., Shirk, S. R., & Potter, C. (2015). Testing two approaches to revictimization prevention among adolescent girls in the child welfare system. *Journal of Adolescent Health, 56*, S33–S39.

DeRosa, R. R., & Rathus, J. H. (2013). Dialectical behavior therapy with adolescents. In J. D. Ford & C. A. Courtois (Eds.), *Treating complex traumatic stress disorders in children and adolescents: Scientific foundations and therapeutic models* (pp. 225–245). New York, NY: Guilford Press.

Dobbs, D. (2012, December 24). A new focus on the "post" in post-traumatic stress. *The New York Times*. Retrieved from http://www.nytimes.com/2012/12/25/science/understanding-the-effects-of-social-environment-on-trauma-victims.html

Durso, L. E., & Gates, G. J. (2012). *Serving our youth: Findings from a national survey of service providers working with lesbian, gay, bisexual, and transgender youth who are homeless or at risk of becoming homeless*. Retrieved from http://williamsinstitute.law.ucla.edu/research/safe-schools-and-youth/serving-our-youth-july-2012

ECPAT USA. (2013). *And boys too*. Retrieved from http://www.ecpatusa.org/wp-content/uploads/2016/02/and-boys-to-report.pdf

Edwards, J. M., Iritani, B. J., & Hallfors, D. D. (2006). Prevalence and correlates of exchanging sex for drugs or money among adolescents in the United States. *Sexually Transmitted Infections, 82*, 354–358. doi:10.1136/sti.2006.020693

Estes, R. J., & Weiner, N. A. (2001). *The commercial sexual exploitation of children in the U.S., Canada and Mexico*. Retrieved from http://www.thenightministry.org/070_facts_figures/030_research_links/060_homeless_youth/CommercialSexualExploitationofChildren.pdf

Farley, M., Cotton, A, Lynne, J., Zumbeck, S., Spiwak, F., Reyes, M., . . . Sezgin, U. (2003). Prostitution and trafficking in nine countries: An update on violence and post-traumatic stress disorder. *Journal of Trauma Practice, 2*(3/4), 33–74.

Farley, M., Schuckman, E., Golding, J. M., Houser, K., Jarrett, L., Qualliotine, P., & Decker, M. (2011). *Comparing sex buyers with men who don't buy sex: "You can have a good time with the servitude" vs. "you're supporting a system of degradation."* Retrieved from http://www.prostitutionresearch.com/pdf/Farleyetal2011ComparingSexBuyers.pdf

Farrell, A. (2012). Improving law enforcement identification and response to human trafficking. In J. Winterdyk, B. Perrin, & P. Reichel (Eds.), *Human trafficking: Exploring the international nature, concerns and complexities* (pp. 181–206). Boca Raton, FL: Taylor & Francis.

Farrell, A., McDevitt, J., & Fahy, S. (2008). *Understanding and improving law enforcement responses to human trafficking.* Retrieved from https://www.ncjrs.gov/pdffiles1/nij/grants/222752.pdf

Farrell, A., McDevitt, J., & Fahy, S. (2010). Where are all the victims? Understanding the determinants of official identification of human trafficking incidents. *Criminology & Public Policy, 9*(2), 201–233.

Farrell, A., McDevitt, J., Pfeffer, R, Fahy, S., Owens, C., Dank, M, & Adams, W. (2012). *Identifying challenges to improve the investigation and prosecution of state and local human trafficking cases.* Retrieved from https://www.ncjrs.gov/pdffiles1/nij/grants/238795.pdf

Farrell, A., & Pfeffer, R. (2014). Policing human trafficking: Cultural blinders and organizational barriers. *Annals of the American Academy of Political and Social Science, 653*, 46–64. doi:10.1177/0002716213515835

Farrell, A., Pfeffer, R., & Bright, K. (2015). Police perceptions of human trafficking. *Journal of Crime and Justice, 38*(3), 315–333.

Fassett, B. (2012, February). *Dallas high risk victims model.* Paper presented at the Institute of Medicine Committee on Commercial Sexual Exploitation and Sex Trafficking of Minors in the United States meeting, Washington, DC.

Federal Bureau of Investigation. (2012). *Gang criminal activity expanding into juvenile prostitution.* Retrieved from http://www.fbi.gov/stats-services/publications/2011-national-gang-threat-assessment

Federal Bureau of Investigation. (2014, June 23). *168 juveniles recovered in nationwide operation targeting commercial child sex trafficking.* Retrieved from http://www.fbi.gov/news/pressrel/press-releases/168-juveniles-recovered-in-nationwide-operation-targeting-commercial-child-sex-trafficking

Figlewski, B. M., & Brannon, L. W. (2013). Trafficking and the commercial sexual exploitation of young men and boys. In J. L. Goodman & D. A. Leidholdt (Eds.), *Lawyer's manual on human trafficking: Pursuing justice for*

References 147

victims (pp. 149–166). Supreme Court of the State of New York, Appellate Division, First Department. New York State Judicial Committee on Women in the Courts. Retrieved from https://www.nycourts.gov/ip/womeninthecourts/pdfs/LMHT.pdf

Fink, E., & Segell, L. (2013, February 27). Pimps hit social networks to recruit underage sex workers. *CNN Money*. Retrieved from http://money.cnn.com/2013/02/27/technology/social/pimps-social-networks/

Finkelhor, D., & Jones, L. (2006). Why have child maltreatment and child victimization declined? *Journal of Social Issues, 62*(4), 685–716.

Gangamma, R., Slesnick, N., Toviessi, P., & Serovich, J. (2007). Comparison of HIV risks among gay, lesbian, bisexual and heterosexual homeless youth. *Journal of Youth & Adolescence, 37*, 456–464. doi:10.1007/s10964-007-9171-9

Gay, Lesbian & Straight Education Network. (2011). *2011 National School Climate Survey*. Retrieved from http://www.glsen.org/press/2011-national-school-climate-survey

Goldblatt Grace, L., Starck, M., Potenza, J., Kenney, P. A., & Sheetz, A. H. (2012). Commercial sexual exploitation of children and the school nurse. *Journal of School Nursing, 28*(6), 410–417.

Grant, J. M., Mottet, L. A., Tanis, J., Harrison, J., Herman, J. L., & Keisling, M. (2011). *Injustice at every turn: A report of the National Transgender Discrimination Survey*. Retrieved from http://www.thetaskforce.org/static_html/downloads/reports/reports/ntds_full.pdf

Greenbaum, J., Crawford-Jakubiak, & Committee on Child Abuse & Neglect. (2015). Child sex trafficking and commercial sexual exploitation: Health care needs of victims. *Pediatrics, 135*(3), 566–574.

Grubb, D., & Bennett, K. (2012). The readiness of local law enforcement to engage in US anti-trafficking efforts: An assessment of human trafficking training and knowledge of local, county and state law enforcement agencies in the State of Georgia. *Police Practice and Research, 13*(6), 487–500.

Gwadz, M. V., Gostnell, K., Smolenski, C., Willis, B., Nish, D., Nolan, T. C., ... Ritchie, A. S. (2009). The initiation of homeless youth into the street economy. *Journal of Adolescence, 32*, 357–377.

Hawthorne, M. (2015, June 14). Studies link lead exposure to violence. *York Daily Record*, p. A4.

Hickle, K. E., & Roe-Sepowitz, D. (2014). Putting the pieces back together: A group intervention for sexually exploited adolescent girls. *Social Work with Groups, 37*(2), 99–113. doi:10.1080/01609513.2013.823838

Holger-Ambrose, B., Langmade, C., Edinburgh, L. D., & Saewyc, E. (2013). The illusions and juxtapositions of commercial sexual exploitation emong youth: Identifying effective street-outreach strategies. *Journal of Child Sexual Abuse, 22*, 326–340.

Hom, K. A., & Woods, S. J., (2013). Trauma and its aftermath for commercially sexually exploited women as told by front-line service providers. *Issues in Mental Health Nursing, 34*, 75–81.

Hotaling, N., Burris, A., Johnson, B. J., Bird, Y. M., & Melbye, K. A. (2003). Been there done that: SAGE, a peer leadership model among prostitution survivors. *Journal of Trauma Practice, 2*(3/4), 255–265.

Human Rights Campaign. (2015). *Congress ignores needs of homeless youth in trafficking bill*. Retrieved from http://www.hrc.org/blog/congress-ignores-needs-of-homeless-youth-in-trafficking-bill

Institute of Medicine. (2013). *Confronting commercial sexual exploitation and sex trafficking of minors in the United States*. Washington, DC: National Academies Press.

International Labour Organization. (2012). *ILO global estimate of forced labour 2012: Results and methodology*. Retrieved from http://www.ilo.org/sapfl/Informationresources/ILOPublications/WCMS_182004/lang--en/index.htm

Irazola, S., Williamson, E., Chen, C., Garrett, A., & Clawson, H. J. (2008). *Trafficking of U.S. citizens and legal permanent residents: The forgotten victims and survivors*. Retrieved from http://thehill.com/sites/default/files/ICFI_TraffickingofUSCitizens_0.pdf

Irvine, A. (2010). "We've had three of them": Addressing the invisibility of lesbian, gay, bisexual and gender non-conforming youth in the juvenile justice system. *Columbia Journal of Gender and Law, 19*, 675–701.

Jouvenal, J. (2012, September 14). Leader of underage prostitution ring sentenced to 40 years in prison. *Washington Post*. Retrieved from https://www.washingtonpost.com/local/crime/leader-of-underage-prostitution-ring-sentenced-to-40-years-in-prison/2012/09/14/c74f86f2-fea6-11e1-b153-218509a954e1_story.html

Justice for Victims of Trafficking Act of 2015, Pub. L. 114-22.

Kaiser Family Foundation. (2010). *Generation M2: Media in the lives of 8- to 18-year-olds*. Retrieved from http://kff.org/other/report/generation-m2-media-in-the-lives-of-8-to-18-year-olds/

Kelly, A. (2014, November 15). "I carried his name on my body for nine years": The tattooed trafficking survivors reclaim their past. *The Guardian*

Retrieved from http://www.theguardian.com/global-development/2014/nov/16/sp-the-tattooed-trafficking-survivors-reclaiming-their-past

Kennedy, M. A., Klein, C., Bristowe, J. T. K., Cooper, B. S., & Yuille, J. C. (2007). Routes of recruitment: Pimps' techniques and other circumstances that lead to street prostitution. *Journal of Aggression, Maltreatment and Trauma, 15*(2), 1–19.

Kennedy, M. A., Klein, C., Gorzalka, B. B., & Yuille, J. C. (2004). Attitude change following a diversion program for men who solicit sex. *Journal of Offender Rehabilitation, 40*(1/2), 41–60. doi:10.1300/J076v40n01-03

Kerig, P. K., Wainryb, C., Twali, M. S., & Chaplo, S. D. (2013). America's child soldiers: Toward a research agenda for studying gang-involved youth in the United States. *Journal of Aggression, Maltreatment & Trauma, 22*(7), 773–795. doi:10.1080/10926771.2013.813883

Kliethermes, M., Nanney, R. W., Cohen, J. A., & Mannarino, A. P. (2013). Trauma-focused cognitive-behavioral therapy. In J. D. Ford & C. A. Courtois (Eds.), *Treating complex traumatic stress disorders in children and adolescents: Scientific foundations and therapeutic models* (pp. 184–202). New York, NY: Guilford Press.

Konrad, K., Firk, C., & Uhlhaas, P. J. (2013). Brain development during adolescence: Neuroscientific insights into this developmental period. *Deutsches Ärzteblatt International, 110*(25), 425–431.

Kramer, L. A. (2003). Emotional experiences of performing prostitution. *Journal of Trauma Practice, 2*(3/4), 187–197.

Lalor, K., & McElvaney, R. (2010). Child sexual abuse, links to later sexual exploitation/high-risk sexual behavior, and prevention/treatment programs. *Trauma, Violence, and Abuse, 11*(4), 159–177.

Lankenau, S. E., Clatts, M. C., Welle, D., Goldsamt, L. A., & Gwadz, M. V. (2004). Street careers: Homelessness, drug use and sex work among young men who have sex with men (YMSM). *International Journal of Drug Policy, 16*, 10–18.

Lanktree, C., & Briere, J. (2013). Integrative treatment of complex trauma. In J. D. Ford & C. A. Courtois (Eds.), *Treating complex traumatic stress disorders in children and adolescents: Scientific foundations and therapeutic models* (pp. 143–161). New York, NY: Guilford Press.

Lederer, L. J. (2011). Sold for sex: The link between street gangs and trafficking in persons. *The Protection Project Journal of Human Rights and Civil Society.* Retrieved from http://www.globalcenturion.org/wp-content/uploads/2010/02/Sold-for-Sex-The-Link-between-Street-Gangs-and-Trafficking-in-Persons-1.pdf

Leitch, L., & Snow, M. (2013). *Intervene: Practitioner guide and intake tool.* Vancouver, WA: Shared Hope International.

Lin, C. (2012). Children who run away from foster care: Who are the children and what are the risk factors? *Children and Youth Services Review, 34,* 807–813.

Luby, J., Belden, A., Botteron, K., Marrus, N., Harms, M. P., Babb, C., . . . Barch, D. (2013). The effects of poverty on childhood brain development: The mediating effect of caregiving and stressful life events. *JAMA Pediatrics, 167*(12), 1135–1142.

Macias-Konstantopoulos, W., Munroe, D., Purcell, G., Tester, K., & Burke, T. F. (2015). The commercial sexual exploitation and sex trafficking of minors in the Boston metropolitan area: Experiences and challenges faced by front-line providers and other stakeholders. *Journal of Applied Research on Children, 6*(1), Article 4. Retrieved from http://digitalcommons.library. tmc.edu/childrenatrisk/vol6/iss1/4/

Madhani, A. (2015, July 1). Visa follows MasterCard, cuts off business with Backpage.com. *USA Today.* Retrieved from http://www.usatoday.com/ story/money/2015/07/01/visa-mastercard-stop-business-with-backpage/ 29558315/

Malarek, V. (2011). *The johns: Sex for sale and the men who buy it.* New York, NY: Arcade.

Marcus, A., Horning, A., Curtis, R., Sanson, J., & Thompson, E. (2014). Conflict and agency among sex workers and pimps: A closer look at domestic minor sex trafficking. *Annals of the American Academy of Political and Social Science, 653*(1), 225–246.

McKeen, A., & Blank, S. V. (2014). *The demand side: Traffickers, buyers and gangs* Webinar series offered by Children's Healthcare of Atlanta. http://www. choa.org/csecwebinarmaterials

McMahon-Howard, J., & Reimers, B. (2013). An evaluation of child welfare training program on the commercial sexual exploitation of children (CSEC). *Evaluation and Program Planning, 40,* 1–9.

Mitchell, K. J., Finkelhor, D., & Wolak, J. (2010). Conceptualizing juvenile prostitution as child maltreatment: Findings from the National Juvenile Prostitution Study. *Child Maltreatment, 15*(1), 18–36.

Morley, C. A., & Kohrt, B. A. (2013). Impact of peer support on PTSD, hope, functional impairment: A mixed-methods study of child soldiers in Nepal. *Journal of Aggression, Maltreatment & Trauma, 22*(7), 714–734, doi:10.1080/10926771.2013.813882

Mother pleads guilty in Shaniya Davis' death. (2013, October 18). *WRAL News*. Retrieved from http://www.wral.com/mother-pleads-guilty-in-shaniya-davis-death/13011614/

Mother who tried to sell 13-year-old daughter's virginity for $10,000 faces 15 years in jail. (2012, February 15). *The Daily Mail*. Retrieved from http://www.dailymail.co.uk/news/article-2101130/Mother-tried-sell-13-year-old-daughters-virginity-10-000-sentenced-prison.html

Moxley-Goldsmith, T. (2005). Boys in the basement: Male victims of commercial sexual exploitation. *Update*, 2(1). Retrieved from http://www.ndaa.org/pdf/child_sexual_exploitation_update_volume_2_number_1_2005.pdf

National Public Radio (NPR). (2013). *Finding and stopping child sex trafficking*. Retrieved from http://www.npr.org/templates/story/story.php?storyId=207901614

National Scientific Council on the Developing Child. (2012). *The science of neglect: The persistent absence of responsive care disrupts the developing brain*. Retrieved from http://developingchild.harvard.edu/resources/reports_and_working_papers/working_papers/wp12/

Natisha Hillard pleads guilty to selling baby for sex. (2014, February 7). *Huffington Post*. Retrieved from http://www.huffingtonpost.com/2014/01/27/natisha-hillard-guilty-child-porn-sells-toddler-sex_n_4675036.html

Nixon, K., Tutty, L., Downe, P., Gorkoff, K., & Ursel, J. (2002). The everyday occurrence: Violence in the lives of girls exploited by prostitution. *Violence Against Women, 8*(9), 1016–1043.

Noble, K. G., Houston, S. M., Brito, N. H., Bartsch, H., Kan, E., Kuperman, J. M., . . . Sowell, E. R. (2015). Family income, parental education and brain structure in children and adolescents. *Nature Neuroscience, 18*, 773–778.

OP man sentenced for sex trafficking of child. (2010, May 10). Retrieved from http://www.kctv5.com/story/14784324/op-man-sentenced-for-sex-trafficking-of-child-5-10-2010

Patel, D. (2013, November). *Gang-controlled sexual exploitation: A treatment approach*. Paper presented at Shared Hope Internationals' JuST (Juvenile Sex Trafficking) conference, Washington, DC.

Pedersen, W., & Hegna, K. (2003). Children and adolescents who sell sex: A community study. *Social Science and Medicine, 56*, 135–147.

Pierce, S. (2015, April 2). *Protecting children from human trafficking*. Retrieved from http://humantraffickingsearch.net/wp/protecting-children-from-human-trafficking/

Polaris. (2012). *Increasing awareness and engagement. Annual report 2011.* Retrieved from https://traffickingresourcecenter.org/resources/increasing-awareness-and-engagement-strengthening-national-response-human-trafficking-us

Polaris. (2014). *Human trafficking issue brief: Safe harbor.* Retrieved from https://polarisproject.org/sites/default/files/2015%20Safe%20Harbor%20Issue%20Brief.pdf

Polaris. (2015a). *Law enforcement training on human trafficking.* Retrieved from http://www.polarisproject.org/

Polaris. (2015b). *Congress: Pass the Runaway and Homeless Youth and Trafficking Prevention Act.* Retrieved from http://hq.salsalabs.com/o/5417/p/dia/action3/common/public/index.sjs?action_KEY=19547

Polaris. (2015c). 2014 state ratings on human trafficking laws. Retrieved from https://polarisproject.org/resources/2014-state-ratings-human-trafficking-laws

Raphael, J., & Myers-Powell, B. (2010). From victims to victimizers: Interviews with 25 ex-pimps in Chicago. *DePaul University College of Law.* Retrieved from http://newsroom.depaul.edu/PDF/FAMILY_LAW_CENTER_REPORT-final.pdf

Raphael, J., Reichert, J. A., & Powers, M. (2010). Pimp control and violence: Domestic sex trafficking of Chicago women and girls. *Women & Criminal Justice, 20,* 89–104.

Reichert, J., & Sylwestrzak, A. (2013). National survey of residential programs for victims of sex trafficking. *The Illinois Criminal Justice Information Authority.* Retrieved from http://www.icjia.state.il.us/assets/pdf/researchreports/nsrhvst_101813.pdf

Reid, J. (2013). Rapid assessment exploring impediments to successful prosecutions of sex traffickers of U.S. minors. *Journal of Police and Criminal Psychology, 28,* 75–89. doi:10.1007/s11896-012-9106-6

Reid, J. A. (2014). Entrapment and enmeshment schemes used by sex traffickers. *Sexual Abuse.* Epub ahead of print. doi:10.1177/1079063214544334

Reid, J. A., Huard, J., & Haskell, R. A. (2015). Family-facilitated juvenile sex trafficking. *Journal of Crime and Justice, 38*(3), 361–376. doi:10.1080/0735648X.2014.967965

Reid, J. A., & Jones, S. (2011). Exploited vulnerability: Legal and psychological perspectives on child sex trafficking victims. *Victims & Offenders, 6,* 207–231.

Reid, J. A., & Piquero, A. R. (2014). Age-graded risks for commercial sexual exploitation of male and female youth. *Journal of Interpersonal Violence, 29*(9), 1747–1777.

Renzetti, C. N., Bush, A., Castellanos, M., & Hunt, G. (2015). Does training make a difference? An evaluation of a specialized human trafficking training module for law enforcement officers. *Journal of Crime and Justice*, *38*(3), 334–350.

Roe-Sepowitz, D. (2012). Juvenile entry into prostitution: The role of emotional abuse. *Violence Against Women*, *18*(5), 562–579.

Roe-Sepowitz, D. E., & Gallagher, J. (n.d.). *Prostitution ads on Backpage.com study: Q&A on key findings, research methodology.* Retrieved from https://archive.copp.asu.edu/college-news/pressreleases/prostitution-ads-on-backpage.com-study-q-a-on-key-findings-research-methodology

Roe-Sepowitz, D. E., Hickle, K. E., & Cimino, A. (2012). The impact of abuse history and trauma symptoms on successful completion of a prostitution-exiting program. *Journal of Human Behavior in the Social Environment*, *22*, 65–77.

Roe-Sepowitz, D., Hickle, K., Gallagher, J., Smith, J., & Hedberg, E. (2013). *Invisible offenders: A study estimating online sex customers.* Retrieved from https://traffickingresourcecenter.org/sites/default/files/Study%20Estimating%20Online%20Sex%20Customers%20-%20ASU_0.pdf

Romer, D. (2010). Adolescent risk taking, impulsivity, and brain development: Implications for prevention. *Developmental Psychobiology*, *52*(3), 273–276.

Ross, C. A., Farley, M., & Schwartz, H. L. (2003). Dissociation among women in prostitution. *Journal of Trauma Practice*, *2*(3/4), 199–212.

Salisbury, E. J., & Dabney, J. D. (2011). *Youth victims of domestic minor sex trafficking in Clark County Juvenile Court: Implementing an identification and diversion process.* Retrieved from http://sharedhope.org/wp-content/uploads/2012/09/DMSTCCJC.pdf

Sex Trafficking Survivors United. (2014). *Statement against Amnesty International's suggestion that buying sex is a human right.* Retrieved from http://www.sextraffickingsurvivorsunited.org/statement-against-amnesty-internationals-suggestion-that-buying-sex-is-a-human-right/

Shared Hope International. (2007). *Demand.* Retrieved from http://sharedhope.org/wp-content/uploads/2012/09/DEMAND.pdf/

Shared Hope International. (2009). *The national report on domestic sex trafficking (America's prostituted children).* Retrieved from http://sharedhope.org/wp-content/uploads/2012/09/SHI_National_Report_on_DMST_2009.pdf

Shared Hope International. (2014). *Demanding justice report 2014.* Retrieved from http://sharedhope.org/wp-content/uploads/2014/08/Demanding_Justice_Report_2014.pdf

Shared Hope International. (2015). *Justice for Victims of Trafficking Act: Section-by-section analysis*. Retrieved from http://sharedhope.org/wp-content/up-loads/2015/03/Justice-for-Victims-of-Trafficking-Act-2015_Section-by-Section_Reported-....pdf

Shelton, J. (2015). Transgender youth homelessness: Understanding programmatic barriers through the lens of cisgenderism. *Children and Youth Services Review, 59*, 10–18.

Shively, M., Kliorys, K., Wheeler, K., & Hunt, D. (2012). *A national overview of prostitution and sex trafficking demand reduction efforts*. Retrieved from https://www.ncjrs.gov/pdffiles1/nij/grants/238796.pdf

Smith, H. A. (2014). *Walking prey: How America's youth are vulnerable to sex slavery*. New York, NY: Palgrave Macmillan.

Smith, H. A. (2015a, January 5). How certain efforts to prevent human trafficking are proving to be hurtful. *Elite Daily*. Retrieved from http://holly austinsmith.com/how-certain-efforts-to-prevent-human-trafficking-are-proving-to-be-hurtful/

Smith, H. A. (2015b, February 13). Human trafficking: Do our advocacy efforts dehumanize victims? *Elite Daily*. Retrieved from http://elitedaily.com/news/world/human-trafficking-advocacy-efforts-affecting-problem/916217/

Smith, H. A. (2015c, March 26). Human trafficking: Are we effectively reaching victims? *Huffington Post*. Retrieved from http://www.huffingtonpost.com/holly-austin-smith/human-trafficking-are-we-_b_6946592.html

Smith, J. (2014, April 23). Address the imbalance at the heart of prostitution. *The Guardian*. Retrieved from http://www.theguardian.com/commentis-free/2014/apr/23/uk-buying-sex-illegal-prostitution

Smith, L. W., Herman-Giddens, M. F., & Everette, V. D. (2005). Commercial sexual exploitation of children in advertising. In S. W. Cooper, R. J. Estes, A. P. Giardino, N. D. Kellogg, & V. I. Vieth (Eds.), *Medical, legal, & social science aspects of child sexual exploitation* (pp. 25–57). St. Louis, MO: STM Learning.

Smith, M. (2015, March 18). A new effort to rescue runaways in Chicago. *New York Times*. Retrieved from http://www.nytimes.com/2015/03/19/us/in-chicago-a-new-effort-to-rescue-runaways.html

Sneed, T. (2015, January 14). How big data battles human trafficking. *US News & World Report*. Retrieved from http://www.usnews.com/news/articles/2015/01/14/how-big-data-is-being-used-in-the-fight-against-human-trafficking

Summers, K. (2013, May 19). After sex-trafficking arrests, Backpage.com under fire. *Tampa Bay Times*. Retrieved from http://www.tampabay.com

Swedish Institute. (2010). *Evaluation of the ban on purchase of sexual services.* Retrieved from https://ec.europa.eu/anti-trafficking/sites/antitrafficking/files/the_ban_against_the_purchase_of_sexual_services._an_evaluation_1999-2008_1.pdf

Tsukayama, H. (2015, November 3). Teens spend nearly nine hours every day consuming media. *Washington Post.* Retrieved from http://www.washingtonpost.com

Tucker, A. (2014, June 23). 168 children rescued in sex-trafficking crackdown: FBI. *The Huffington Post.* Retrieved from http://www.huffingtonpost.com/2014/06/23/operation-cross-country_n_5523540.html?utm_hp_ref=tw

Twill, S. E., Green, D. M., & Traylor, A. (2010). A descriptive study on sexually exploited children in residential treatment. *Child & Youth Care Forum, 39,* 187–199.

Tyler, K. A., Hoyt, D. R., & Whitbeck, L. B. (2000). The effects of early sexual abuse on later sexual victimization among female homeless and runaway adolescents. *Journal of Interpersonal Violence, 15,* 235–250.

United Nations Office on Drugs and Crime. (2004). *United Nations Convention against Transnational Organized Crime and the Protocols thereto.* Retrieved from http://www.unodc.org/documents/treaties/UNTOC/Publications/TOC%20Convention/TOCebook-e.pdf

United Nations Office on Drugs and Crime. (n.d.). *United Nations Convention against Transnational Organized Crime and the Protocols thereto.* Retrieved from http://www.unodc.org/unodc/en/treaties/CTOC/index.html

Urbina, I. (2009, October 25). Recession drives surge in youth runaways. *New York Times.* Retrieved from http://www.nytimes.com/2009/10/26/us/26runaway.html

US Department of Health and Human Services. (2012). *Fact sheet: Human trafficking.* Retrieved from http://www.acf.hhs.gov/programs/orr/resource/fact-sheet-human-trafficking

US Department of Health and Human Services. (2015, February 9). Adoption and foster care analysis and reporting system. *Federal Register, 80*(26), 7132–7221. Retrieved from https://www.federalregister.gov/articles/2015/02/09/2015-02354/adoption-and-foster-care-analysis-and-reporting-system

US Department of Justice. (2009, December 18). *Final defendant pleads guilty to sex trafficking of a child.* Retrieved from http://www.justice.gov/usao/mow/news2009/mikoloyck.ple.htm

US Department of Justice. (2012). *Gang leader sentenced to 40 years for leading juvenile sex trafficking ring.* Retrieved from http://www.justice.gov/archive/usao/vae/news/2012/09/20120914stromnr.html

Walker Pettigrew, W. (2013). Hearing on protecting vulnerable children: Preventing sex trafficking of youth in foster care. *Testimony to the House Ways and Means Committee, Subcommittee on Human Resources*. Retrieved from http://waysandmeans.house.gov/hearing-on-preventing-and-addressing-sex-trafficking-of-youth-in-foster-care/

Wells, M., Mitchell, K. J., & Ji, K. (2012). Exploring the role of the internet in juvenile prostitution cases coming to the attention of law enforcement. *Journal of Child Sexual Abuse, 21*, 327–342.

West, A., & Loeffler, D. N. (2015). Understanding victim resistance: An exploratory study of the experiences of service providers working with child victims of child trafficking. *Journal of Applied Research on Children, 6*(1), Article 5. Retrieved from http://digitalcommons.library.tmc.edu/cgi/viewcontent.cgi?article=1231&context=childrenatrisk

Westerman, A. S. (2014, December 23). *New hospital protocol aims to help identify victims of human trafficking*. Retrieved from http://cnsmaryland.org/2014/12/19/new-hospital-protocol-aims-to-help-identify-victims-of-human-trafficking/

Whittle, H., Hamilton-Giachritsis, C., Beech, A., & Collings, G. (2013). A review of online grooming: Characteristics and concerns. *Aggression and Violent Behavior, 18*, 62–70.

Widom, C., & Kuhns, J. B. (1996). Childhood victimization and subsequent risk for promiscuity, prostitution, and teenage pregnancy: A prospective study. *American Journal of Public Health, 87*(11), 1607–1612.

Williamson, C., & Cluse-Tolar, T. (2002). Pimp-controlled prostitution: Still an integral part of street life. *Violence Against Women, 8*(9), 1074–1092.

Williamson, C., & Prior, M. (2009). Domestic minor sex trafficking: A network of underground players in the Midwest. *Journal of Child & Adolescent Trauma. 2*, 46–61.

Willoughby, T., Good, M., Adachi, P. J. C., Hamza, C., & Tavernier, R. (2013). Examining the link between adolescent brain development and risk taking from a social-developmental perspective. *Brain and Cognition, 83*, 315–323.

Wilson, E. C., Garofalo, R., Harris, R. D., Herrick, A., Martinez, M., Martinez, J., . . . The Transgender Advisory Committee and the Adolescent Medicine Trials Network for HIV/AIDS Interventions. (2009). Transgender female youth and sex work: HIV risk and a comparison of life factors related to engagement in sex work. *AIDS Behavior, 13*, 902–913. doi:10.1007/s10461-008-9508-8

Wilson, B. D. M., & Kastanis, A. A. (2015). Sexual and gender minority disproportionality and disparities in child welfare: A population-based study. *Children and Youth Services Review, 58*, 11–17.

Wilson, H. W., & Widom, C. S. (2010). The role of youth problem behaviors in the path from child abuse and neglect to prostitution: A prospective examination. *Journal of Research on Adolescence, 20*(1), 210–236. doi:10.1111/j.1532-7795.2009.00624.x

Woolf, W. (2013, November). *Gang-controlled DMST: An overview.* Paper presented at Shared Hope International's JuST (Juvenile Sex Trafficking) conference, Washington, DC.

Wright, J. P., Dietrich, K. N., Ris, M. D., Hornung, R. W., Wessel, S. D., Lanphear, B. P., . . . Rae, M. N. (2008). Association of prenatal and childhood blood lead concentrations with criminal arrests in early adulthood. *PLoS Medicine, 5*(5), 732–740.

Yarbrough, J. (2012). *LGBTQ youth permanency.* Retrieved from http://www.hunter.cuny.edu/socwork/nrcfcpp/info_services/download/LGBTQ%20Youth%20Permanency_JesseYarbrough.pdf

Ybarra, M. L., Strasburger, V. C., & Mitchell, K. J. (2014). Sexual media exposure, sexual behavior, and sexual violence victimization in adolescence. *Clinical Pediatrics, 53*(13), 1239–1247.

Young, J. C., & Widom, C. S. (2014). Long-term effects of child abuse and neglect on emotion processing in adulthood. *Child Abuse & Neglect, 38*, 1369–1381.

Index